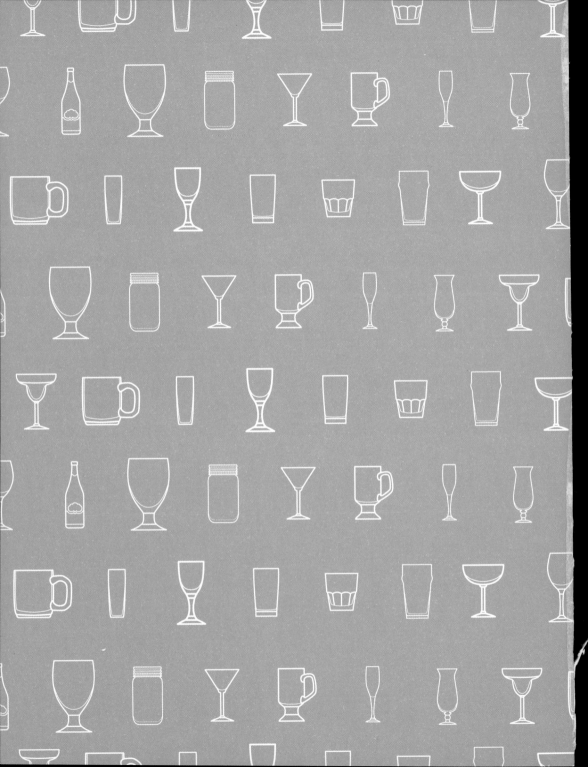

EASY COCKTAILS

OVER 150 DRINKS, ALL MADE WITH
FOUR INGREDIENTS OR LESS

13-Digit ISBN: 978-1-64643-101-4
10-Digit ISBN: 1-64643-101-4

This book may be ordered by mail from the publisher. Please include $5.99 for postage and handling. Please support your local bookseller first!

Books published by Cider Mill Press Book Publishers are available at special discounts for bulk purchases in the United States by corporations, institutions, and other organizations. For more information, please contact the publisher.

Cider Mill Press Book Publishers
"Where good books are ready for press"

PO Box 454
12 Spring Street
Kennebunkport, Maine 04046

Visit us online!
cidermillpress.com

Typography: Berthold Akzidenz Grotesk and Trump Gothic Pro
Image Credits: Pages 14, 33, 34, 38, 41, 42, 49, 53, 54, 57, 58, 61, 62, 65, 85, 86, 101, 125, 126, 129, 130, 134, 137, 153, 159, 163, 167, 172, 179, 188, 191, 192, 196, 203, 204, 207, 208, 229, 234, 238, 241, 253, 257, 258, 275, 276, 279, 284, 288, 292, 295, 296, 299, 300, 304, 307, 311, 319, 323, 327, 331, 338, 342, 347, 348, 363, 365, 367 courtesy of Cider Mill Press. All other images used under official license from Shutterstock.

Printed in China
3 4 5 6 7 8 9 0

EASY COCKTAILS

OVER 150 DRINKS, ALL MADE WITH
FOUR INGREDIENTS OR LESS

CIDER MILL
PRESS

BOOK
PUBLISHERS
KENNEBUNKPORT, MAINE

Contents

Introduction

In a relatively short period of time, the modern culinary movement has accomplished miraculous things, flooding the mainstream with new and exciting flavors. Unsurprisingly, cocktails are among the items that this rising tide has lifted, with passionate mixologists everywhere intent on showing off what a practiced hand and a bit of imagination can pull off. All of a sudden, it seems like every restaurant has a cocktail program filled with drinks built on bespoke syrups and tinctures.

That's a revolution from where things stood during the dark days of the '80s, when a request for a cocktail was typically followed by someone fumbling around beneath the bar for a cocktail recipe booklet, and a finished product that featured an unhealthy reliance on some sugary, prefab mix.

We're in a better place, no doubt. But this drive for constant innovation (and the quest for eyes and likes on Instagram) has caused something of an exclusive air to settle around the craft of cocktail making, causing the average person to feel as though they have no business trying to make their own cocktails at home.

That, simply, is nonsense. Many cocktails—and nearly all of the classic ones—are straightforward enough that they could be fashioned (this is not to say mastered—mastery of some, such as the Martini, can evade even a lifetime of dedication) by a complete novice with a quick trip to the liquor store and materials on-hand in every house. Seriously. It no doubt helps to have tools specifically designed for cocktail making—jiggers, a mixing glass, bar spoon, cocktail shaker, and Hawthorne strainer—but one could get entirely passable results using a mason jar, its lid, and a fork.

This book is intent on returning cocktail making to its unfussy, enjoyable, and accessible roots in order to provide your home bar a solid foundation. With its focus on simple recipes consisting of four or less ingredients, it becomes easy to understand how the various elements function and interact with each other, insights that will increase your enjoyment of the resulting cocktail, and provide you with the confidence and feel necessary to come up with your own bespoke concoctions if the mood should strike.

There's a tendency to associate an embrace of simplicity with an acceptance of less-than-stellar products. To ensure that this unfortunate association doesn't enter your practice, here are a few things helpful tips to keep in mind:

1. Ice is just as important as the quality of the liquor you are using. Do your best to use freshly made cubes, and consider keeping a set of ice trays in a resealable plastic bag and reserving them specifically for cocktail ice. You definitely don't want ice that smells like a batch of stew when mixing up a Martini.

2. Fresh juices will always be better than what comes in a bottle or carton. For lime and lemon juice, the difference is so large that one would be wise to categorize fresh as essential.

3. Steering clear of the bottom shelf at the liquor store is paramount. Working with subpar ingredients is counterproductive, and no amount of skill will manage to lift them to a worthwhile level.

Whiskey

Old Fashioned

As the go-to drink for the stylish, and extremely thirsty, Don Draper on the lauded TV show *Mad Men*, the Old Fashioned lost the extraneous elements—club soda is just one—that had been appended to it over the years, returned to its roots, and became the quintessential whiskey cocktail.

1. Place the sugar, bitters, and water in a double rocks glass and stir until the sugar has dissolved.

2. Fill the glass with ice, add the whiskey, and stir until chilled. Express the strip of lemon zest over the cocktail, drop it into the glass, and finish the cocktail with the maraschino cherry.

1 TEASPOON CASTER SUGAR

2 TO 3 DASHES OF BITTERS

DASH OF WATER

2 OZ. BOURBON OR RYE WHISKEY

1 STRIP OF LEMON PEEL,
1 MARASCHINO CHERRY,
FOR GARNISH

GLASSWARE:
DOUBLE ROCKS GLASS

1 OZ. BOURBON

1 OZ. CAMPARI

1 OZ. SWEET VERMOUTH

1 ORANGE TWIST, FOR GARNISH

GLASSWARE:
ROCKS GLASS

Boulevardier

The Negroni's surge in popularity makes most think that this drink is a riff, but it stands in a universe all its own. It's also quite good with a smoky Scotch in place of the bourbon.

1. Place the bourbon, Campari, and vermouth in a mixing glass, fill it two-thirds of the way with ice, and stir until chilled.

2. Strain into a rocks glass filled with ice and garnish with the orange twist.

Manhattan

Bourbon usually gets the call in modern versions of this drink, but its name suggests that the rye whiskey beloved in New York during the 19th century is the correct choice.

1. Chill a cocktail glass in the freezer.

2. Place the whiskey, vermouth, and bitters in a mixing glass, fill it two-thirds of the way with ice, and stir until chilled.

3. Strain into the cocktail glass and garnish with the maraschino cherry.

2 OZ. RYE WHISKEY

⅔ OZ. SWEET VERMOUTH

2 DROPS OF AROMATIC BITTERS

1 MARASCHINO CHERRY, FOR GARNISH

GLASSWARE:
COCKTAIL GLASS

4 FRESH MINT LEAVES

1 TEASPOON CASTER SUGAR

SPLASH OF WATER

2 OZ. BOURBON

1 SPRIG OF FRESH MINT,
FOR GARNISH

GLASSWARE:
HIGHBALL GLASS

Mint Julep

This drink is permanently associated with Kentucky, both due to the Kentucky Derby, where it became the official beverage in 1938, and because of the bourbon that the state is renowned for producing.

1. Place the mint leaves, sugar, and water in a highball glass and muddle.

2. Fill the glass with crushed ice and stir until chilled.

3. Garnish with the sprig of mint.

Rob Roy

There's a lot of room to play with in the Scotch-centered take on the Manhattan, so make sure you don't shy away from experimenting with different Scotches until you land on your favorite.

1. **Add the Scotch, vermouth, and bitters to a mixing glass, fill it two-thirds of the way with ice, and stir until chilled.**

2. **Strain into a cocktail glass and garnish with the maraschino cherry.**

2 OZ. SCOTCH WHISKY

1 OZ. SWEET VERMOUTH

2 DROPS OF ANGOSTURA BITTERS

1 MARASCHINO CHERRY, FOR GARNISH

GLASSWARE: COCKTAIL GLASS

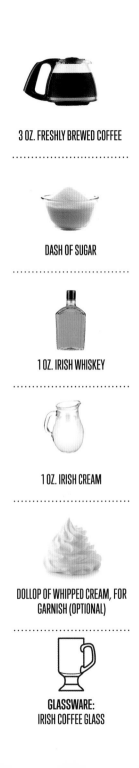

3 OZ. FRESHLY BREWED COFFEE

DASH OF SUGAR

1 OZ. IRISH WHISKEY

1 OZ. IRISH CREAM

DOLLOP OF WHIPPED CREAM, FOR
GARNISH (OPTIONAL)

GLASSWARE:
IRISH COFFEE GLASS

Irish Coffee

One of the rare cocktails beloved by everyone from connoisseurs to neophytes.

1. Pour the coffee into an Irish coffee glass, add the sugar, and stir until the sugar has dissolved.

2. Stir in the whiskey and Irish cream. If desired, garnish with a dollop of whipped cream.

Brother Sparrow

Sweet, tart, and just spicy enough to make each sip a memorable journey.

1. Add the whiskey and lemonade to a double rocks glass filled with ice, stir until chilled, and top with the cranberry juice.

2 OZ. RYE WHISKEY

4 OZ. LEMONADE

2 OZ. CRANBERRY JUICE

GLASSWARE:
DOUBLE ROCKS GLASS

2 OZ. SINGLE-MALT WHISKY

1 OZ. AVERNA AMARO

2 OZ. DRY SPARKLING WINE

GLASSWARE:
CHAMPAGNE FLUTE

Love & Happiness

This classy, refreshing, and complex serve is a tribute to one of Al Green's very best songs.

1. Chill a champagne flute in the freezer.

2. Place the whisky and amaro in a mixing glass, fill it two-thirds of the way with ice, and stir until chilled.

3. Strain into the chilled champagne flute and top with the sparkling wine.

The Third Man

Finding a single-malt where one would expect a gin to be is far from the only surprise in this cocktail.

1. Place all of the ingredients in a cocktail shaker, fill it two-thirds of the way with ice, and shake until chilled.

2. Strain into a rocks glass.

2 OZ. SINGLE-MALT WHISKY

¾ OZ. ST-GERMAIN

¾ OZ. FRESH LEMON JUICE

1 EGG WHITE

GLASSWARE:
ROCKS GLASS

1½ OZ. RYE WHISKEY

4 OZ. ROOT BEER

3 DASHES OF ABSINTHE

1 LEMON WEDGE, FOR GARNISH

GLASSWARE:
COLLINS GLASS

Slipping Into Darkness

This one is light, but packs a surprising punch.

1. Add the whiskey, root beer, and absinthe to a Collins glass filled with ice, stir until chilled, and garnish with the lemon wedge.

SIMPLE SYRUP

Named due to its humble components and the east of making it, there is nothing basic about the role simple syrup plays in cocktail making. Just place equal parts sugar and water in a saucepan, stir as it comes to a boil in order to help the sugar dissolve, and then let it cool.

Whether it is there to offset the lemon or lime juice, allow a tucked-away flavor to surface, or add body and viscosity to a drink, the simple syrup definitively transcends its modest construction.

It is also one of the easiest ways to add flavors to your cocktails. Add 1 tablespoon of an extract, fresh herbs, honey or your preferred sweetener, or 2 teabags to the syrup to easily customize it.

Simca

Go for the smokiest whisky you can handle here, as the syrup, lemon juice, and Luxardo shine brightly amidst all that murk.

1. Place the whisky, lemon juice, syrup, and Luxardo in a cocktail shaker, fill it two-thirds of the way with ice, and shake until chilled.

2. Strain over ice into a rocks glass and garnish with the maraschino cherries.

1½ OZ. SINGLE-MALT WHISKY

1 OZ. FRESH LEMON JUICE

¼ OZ. SIMPLE SYRUP
(SEE SIDEBAR)

¼ OZ. LUXARDO MARASCHINO
LIQUEUR

2 MARASCHINO CHERRIES,
FOR GARNISH

GLASSWARE:
ROCKS GLASS

2 OZ. THE FAMOUS GROUSE
SCOTCH WHISKY

¾ OZ. SIMPLE SYRUP
(SEE PAGE 30)

¾ OZ. FRESH LEMON JUICE

¼ OZ. DRY RED WINE

1 ORANGE WHEEL, FOR GARNISH

GLASSWARE:
ROCKS GLASS

New York Sour

Aficionados may find it hard to believe, but The Famous Grouse is the No. 1 whisky in Scotland, the mecca of whisky. Its soft and sweet taste makes it a natural for cocktails.

1. Place the Scotch, syrup, and lemon juice in a cocktail shaker, fill it two-thirds of the way with ice, and shake until chilled.

2. Strain into a rocks glass filled with ice and float the wine on top by pouring it over the back of a spoon.

3. Garnish with the orange wheel.

Bushwick

A lovely riff on one of the original recipes for the Brooklyn, altering the ratio of rye to vermouth.

1. Place all of the ingredients in a mixing glass, fill it two-thirds of the way with ice, and stir until chilled.

2. Strain into a coupe.

2 OZ. RYE WHISKEY

¾ OZ. SWEET VERMOUTH

¼ OZ. LUXARDO MARASCHINO LIQUEUR

¼ OZ. AMER PICON

GLASSWARE:
COUPE

2 OZ. RYE WHISKEY

½ OZ. CYNAR

¾ OZ. SWEET VERMOUTH

2 MARASCHINO CHERRIES,
FOR GARNISH

GLASSWARE:
COCKTAIL GLASS

Little Italy

Fans of the Manhattan will want to give this one a go as the spicy richness of the Cynar is lovely beside the rye.

1. Chill a cocktail glass in the freezer.

2. Place the rye, Cynar, and vermouth in a mixing glass, fill it two-thirds of the way with ice, and stir until chilled.

3. Strain into the chilled glass and garnish with the cherries.

Margot Tenenbaum

The Zucca Rabarbaro makes this cocktail as enigmatic as it is brilliant.

1. Place all of the ingredients in a cocktail shaker, fill it two-thirds of the way with ice, and shake until chilled.

2. Strain over one large ice cube into a rocks glass.

2 OZ. BOURBON

¾ OZ. FRESH LEMON JUICE

½ OZ. HONEY SYRUP (SEE PAGE 30)

½ OZ. ZUCCA RABARBARO AMARO

GLASSWARE:
ROCKS GLASS

2 OZ. TENNESSEE WHISKEY

½ OZ. FRESH LEMON JUICE

½ OZ. SIMPLE SYRUP
(SEE PAGE 30)

2 DASHES OF ORANGE BITTERS

1 LEMON WHEEL, FOR GARNISH

GLASSWARE:
COUPE

Tennessee Voodoo

Tennessee whiskey, which is filtered through sugar maple charcoal after the distilling process, has established itself as a distinctive branch of the whiskey tree. Watch for it to pick up considerable momentum over the course of the decade.

1. Place the whiskey, lemon juice, syrup, and bitters in a cocktail shaker, fill it two-thirds of the way with ice, and shake until chilled.

2. Strain over ice into a coupe and garnish with the lemon wheel.

Muleskinner Blues

One of Dolly's best gets honored in this variation on the Moscow Mule.

1. Add the whiskey, lime juice, and ginger beer to a copper mug filled with ice and stir until chilled.

2. Garnish with the lime wheel and the sprig of mint.

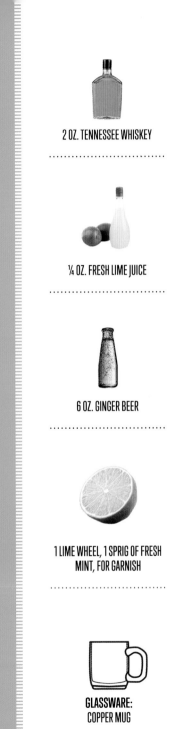

2 OZ. TENNESSEE WHISKEY

¼ OZ. FRESH LIME JUICE

6 OZ. GINGER BEER

1 LIME WHEEL, 1 SPRIG OF FRESH MINT, FOR GARNISH

GLASSWARE:
COPPER MUG

1 OZ. TENNESSEE WHISKEY

¾ OZ. SWEET VERMOUTH

¾ OZ. CHERRY HEERING

1 OZ. FRESH ORANGE JUICE

1 ORANGE WHEEL, FOR GARNISH

GLASSWARE:
COCKTAIL GLASS

Let It Go

The king of Tennessee whiskies—Jack Daniel's—has what you're looking for in this cocktail.

1. Place the whiskey, vermouth, Cherry Heering, and orange juice in a cocktail shaker, fill it two-thirds of the way with ice, and shake until chilled.

2. Strain into a cocktail glass and garnish with the orange wheel.

Pomegranate Smash

The tannins in pomegranate juice cut against its natural sweetness with tartness, allowing it to anchor this cocktail.

1. Place the bourbon, juices, and honey in a cocktail shaker, fill it two-thirds of the way with ice, and shake until chilled.

2. Strain over ice into a tumbler and garnish with the pomegranate seeds.

2 OZ. BOURBON

1 OZ. POMEGRANATE JUICE

½ OZ. FRESH LEMON JUICE

½ OZ. HONEY

POMEGRANATE SEEDS, FOR GARNISH

GLASSWARE: TUMBLER

1 OZ. FRESH LEMON JUICE

1 TEASPOON CASTER SUGAR

1½ OZ. BOURBON

CLUB SODA, TO TOP

1 LEMON SLICE,
1 MARASCHINO CHERRY,
FOR GARNISH

GLASSWARE:
HIGHBALL GLASS

Summer Came Early

It's a Collins with bourbon sliding into the starring role, lending a welcome freshness to the summer circuit.

1. Place the lemon juice and sugar in a highball glass and stir until the sugar has dissolved. Add ice and the bourbon and top with the club soda.

2. Stir gently and garnish with the slice of lemon and the cherry.

Blackberry Pie

The modern culinary revolution has rediscovered the affinity between berries and fresh herbs, and this cocktail is just another beneficiary.

1. Place the blackberries and sage in a cocktail shaker and muddle.

2. Add ice along with the syrup and bourbon and shake until chilled.

3. Strain over ice into a tumbler and garnish with an additional blackberry and another sprig of sage.

2 BLACKBERRIES, PLUS 1 FOR GARNISH

1 SPRIG OF FRESH SAGE, PLUS 1 FOR GARNISH

½ OZ. DEMERARA SYRUP (SEE PAGE 30)

2 OZ. BOURBON

GLASSWARE: TUMBLER GLASS

1½ OZ. BOURBON

· ·

½ OZ. SWEET VERMOUTH

· ·

½ OZ. BLACKBERRY BRANDY

· ·

GLASSWARE:
COUPE

Vibes Is Right

Blackberry brandy doesn't make its way into many cocktails, but after this you'll wonder why.

1. Place the ingredients in a cocktail shaker, fill it two-thirds of the way with ice, and shake until chilled.

2. Strain into a coupe.

Hissing of Summer Lawns

As fresh and calming as the wind following an evening thunderstorm.

1. Place the lemon juice, basil, and syrup in a rocks glass and muddle.

2. Add the rye along with ice, stir until chilled, and garnish with additional basil.

1 OZ. FRESH LEMON JUICE

6 FRESH BASIL LEAVES, PLUS MORE FOR GARNISH

1 OZ. SIMPLE SYRUP (SEE PAGE 30)

2 OZ. RYE WHISKEY

GLASSWARE:
ROCKS GLASS

2 OZ. RYE WHISKEY

½ OZ. BÉNÉDICTINE

½ OZ. SWEET VERMOUTH

4 DASHES OF ANGOSTURA BITTERS

GLASSWARE:
COCKTAIL GLASS

Preakness

Flavored by 56 herbs and spices, Bénédictine is a journey all by itself. Pair it with a good rye, and you're off to the races.

1. Place the ingredients in a cocktail shaker, fill it two-thirds of the way with ice, and shake until chilled.

2. Strain into a cocktail glass.

Frisco

The dash of orange bitters is key to keeping this from becoming a little too sweet.

1. Place the ingredients in a cocktail shaker, fill it two-thirds of the way with ice, and shake until chilled.

2. Strain into a cocktail glass.

2 OZ. RYE WHISKEY

1 OZ. FRESH LEMON JUICE

SPLASH OF BÉNÉDICTINE

DASH OF ORANGE BITTERS

GLASSWARE:
COCKTAIL GLASS

1¾ OZ. BOURBON

¾ OZ. AVERNA AMARO

¼ OZ. STREGA

2 DASHES OF PEYCHAUD'S BITTERS

1 STRIP OF ORANGE PEEL,
FOR GARNISH

GLASSWARE:
ROCKS GLASS

Black Philip

One for those who want to live deliciously.

1. Place the bourbon, amaro, Strega, and bitters in a mixing glass, fill it two-thirds of the way with ice, and stir until chilled.

2. Strain over ice into a rocks glass and garnish with the strip of orange peel.

Night Fever

Between the rye and Domaine de Canton, this cocktail's got quite a kick.

1. Add the rye, vermouth, Domaine de Canton, and bitters to a mixing glass, fill it two-thirds of the way with ice, and stir until chilled.

2. Strain over one large ice cube into a rocks glass and garnish with the strip of lemon peel.

1¼ OZ. RYE WHISKEY

¾ OZ. SWEET VERMOUTH

½ OZ. DOMAINE DE CANTON

DASH OF ANGOSTURA BITTERS

1 STRIP OF LEMON PEEL, FOR GARNISH

GLASSWARE: ROCKS GLASS

1½ OZ. BOURBON

¾ OZ. HONEY SYRUP (SEE PAGE 30)

½ OZ. FRESH LEMON JUICE

DASH OF TABASCO

1 STRIP OF LEMON PEEL,
FOR GARNISH

GLASSWARE:
ROCKS GLASS

Play the Ghost

The honey takes care of the Tabasco's spice, allowing its deep flavor to transform this cocktail.

1. Add the bourbon, syrup, lemon juice, and Tabasco to a cocktail shaker, fill it two-thirds of the way with ice, and shake vigorously.

2. Strain over ice into a rocks glass and garnish with the strip of lemon peel.

Dwight's Friend

The orange bitters are the key to keeping this one in line, so don't hesitate to vary the amount you use to get this one tailored to your taste.

1. Place the bourbon, Kahlúa, and bitters in a mixing glass, fill it two-thirds of the way with ice, and stir until chilled.

2. Strain into a rocks glass filled with ice and garnish with the orange slice.

2 OZ. BOURBON

½ OZ. KAHLÚA

2 DASHES OF ORANGE BITTERS

1 ORANGE SLICE, FOR GARNISH

GLASSWARE:
ROCKS GLASS

1 OZ. BOURBON

....

1 OZ. LEMONADE

....

1 OZ. HONEY SYRUP (SEE PAGE 30)

....

¼ OZ. FRESH LEMON JUICE

....

**1 STRIP OF LEMON PEEL,
FRESH MINT LEAVES, FOR GARNISH**

....

**GLASSWARE:
ROCKS GLASS**

Looking Glass

A cooled-down toddy that will serve you well once the temperature starts to rise.

1. Place the bourbon, lemonade, syrup, and lemon juice in a cocktail shaker, fill it two-thirds of the way with ice, and shake until chilled.

2. Strain over ice into a rocks glass and garnish with the strip of lemon peel and mint leaves.

Ice Age

For those Sundays when a cup of spiked hot coffee just won't do.

1. Add all of the ingredients to a rocks glass filled with ice and stir until chilled.

SPLASH OF SIMPLE SYRUP
(SEE PAGE 30)

DASH OF PEYCHAUD'S BITTERS

2 OZ. BOURBON

4 OZ. ICED COFFEE

GLASSWARE:
ROCKS GLASS

2 OZ. BOURBON

4 OZ. WHOLE MILK

DASH OF SIMPLE SYRUP
(SEE PAGE 30)

2 DROPS OF PURE VANILLA
EXTRACT

FRESHLY GRATED NUTMEG,
FOR GARNISH

GLASSWARE:
COUPE

At the Mercy of Inertia

Regardless of your stance on deserty drinks, you can't help giving in to this one.

1. Place the bourbon, milk, syrup, and vanilla extract in a cocktail shaker, fill it two-thirds of the way with ice, and shake until chilled.

2. Strain into a coupe and top with a dash of nutmeg.

Walk the Night

Your search for a favorite drink just may resolve itself here.

1. Place the rye, cranberry juice, syrup, and bitters in a cocktail shaker, fill it two-thirds of the way with ice, and shake until chilled.

2. Strain over one large ice cube into a tumbler and garnish with the maraschino cherry.

2 OZ. RYE WHISKEY

2 OZ. CRANBERRY JUICE

SPLASH OF SIMPLE SYRUP (SEE PAGE 30)

DASH OF ANGOSTURA BITTERS

1 MARASCHINO CHERRY, FOR GARNISH

GLASSWARE: TUMBLER

2 OZ. BLENDED SCOTCH WHISKY

½ OZ. FRESH LEMON JUICE

¼ OZ. SIMPLE SYRUP
(SEE PAGE 30)

BOILING WATER, TO TOP

1 LEMON WEDGE, 1 CINNAMON
STICK, FOR GARNISH

GLASSWARE:
IRISH COFFEE GLASS

Hot Toddy

Some people believe tea has to be in a Hot Toddy. But when you're working with something as delicious and unique Scotch, you want that flavor out front, not doing battle with some other potent element.

1. Place the Scotch, lemon juice, syrup, and water in an Irish Coffee glass and stir to combine.

2. Garnish with the lemon wedge and the cinnamon stick.

Godfather

Don't hesitate to tinker with the amount of amaretto used here—you want just enough to temper the Scotch to your liking, and it's very easy for this nutty liqueur to steal the show.

1. Place the Scotch and amaretto in a mixing glass, fill it two-thirds of the way with ice, and stir until chilled.

2. Strain over ice into a rocks glass and garnish with the orange twist.

2 OZ. BLENDED SCOTCH WHISKY

⅔ OZ. AMARETTO

1 ORANGE TWIST, FOR GARNISH

GLASSWARE:
ROCKS GLASS

1½ OZ. BLENDED SCOTCH WHISKY

½ OZ. DRAMBUIE

1 LEMON TWIST, FOR GARNISH

GLASSWARE:
ROCKS GLASS

Rusty Nail

It makes sense that the Rusty Nail was one of Rat Pack's signature cocktails, as it carries the suave take on hard living that they are famous for.

1. Place the Scotch and Drambuie in a mixing glass, fill it two-thirds of the way with ice, and stir until chilled.

2. Strain over ice into a rocks glass and garnish with the lemon twist.

Gin

3 OZ. LONDON DRY GIN

....

½ OZ. DRY VERMOUTH

....

1 LEMON TWIST, FOR GARNISH

....

Martini

A cocktail one could spend a life with, as noted by American historian Bernard DeVoto, who once said, "It is one of the happiest marriages on earth, and one of the shortest lived."

1. Chill a cocktail glass in the freezer.

2. Place the gin and vermouth in a mixing glass, fill it two-thirds of the way with ice, and stir until chilled.

3. Strain into the chilled glass and garnish with a lemon twist.

GLASSWARE:
COCKTAIL GLASS

Tom Collins

One of history's most enduring cocktails can be made with Old Tom gin or the citrus-forward London Dry.

1. Fill a Collins glass with ice and place it in the freezer.

2. Place the gin, syrup, and lemon juice in a cocktail shaker, fill it two-thirds of the way with ice, and shake until chilled.

3. Strain into the chilled Collins glass and top with the club soda.

4. Garnish with the lemon wheel and cherry.

2 OZ. OLD TOM GIN

1 OZ. SIMPLE SYRUP (SEE PAGE 30)

¾ OZ. FRESH LEMON JUICE

CLUB SODA, TO TOP

1 LEMON WHEEL, 1 MARASCHINO CHERRY, FOR GARNISH

GLASSWARE:
COLLINS GLASS

2½ OZ. GIN

2½ OZ. TONIC WATER

SPLASH OF FRESH LIME JUICE

1 LIME WEDGE, FOR GARNISH

GLASSWARE:
ROCKS GLASS

Gin & Tonic

Spring for a quality tonic, such as Fever Tree, when you're in the mood for this summer standby.

1. Fill a rocks glass with ice, add the gin and tonic water, and stir until chilled.

2. Top with the lime juice and garnish with the lime wedge.

Negroni

As Kingsley Amis, the great English author and spirits aficionado, once said of the Negroni, "It has the power, rare with drinks and indeed with anything else, of cheering you up."

1. Place the Campari, sweet vermouth, and gin in a mixing glass, fill the glass two-thirds of the way with ice, and stir until chilled.

2. Strain the cocktail over ice into a rocks glass and garnish with the orange slice.

⅔ OZ. CAMPARI

⅔ OZ. SWEET VERMOUTH

2 OZ. GIN

1 ORANGE SLICE, FOR GARNISH

GLASSWARE:
RCOKS GLASS

1 EGG WHITE

2 OZ. GIN

1 OZ. COINTREAU

1 OZ. FRESH LEMON JUICE

GLASSWARE:
COUPE

White Lady

The original recipe for the White Lady likely belongs to the famed bartender Harry MacElhone, who created the drink in 1919 while working at Ciro's Club in London, and then further refined it after he went to Paris to build his legend.

1. Chill a coupe in the freezer.

2. Place all of the ingredients in a cocktail shaker containing no ice and dry shake for 20 seconds. Add ice to the shaker and shake until chilled.

3. Strain into the chilled glass.

Bramble

This modern classic comes courtesy of Dick Bradsell, the legendary London bartender.

1. Place the gin, lemon juice, and syrup in a cocktail shaker, fill it two-thirds of the way with ice, and shake until chilled.

2. Strain into a rocks glass filled with crushed ice, lace the crème de mure on top of the cocktail, and garnish with a blackberry or raspberry.

2 OZ. GIN

1 OZ. FRESH LEMON JUICE

½ OZ. SIMPLE SYRUP
(SEE PAGE 30)

½ OZ. CRÈME DE MURE, TO TOP

1 RASPBERRY OR BLACKBERRY,
FOR GARNISH

GLASSWARE:
ROCKS GLASS

2 OZ. LONDON DRY GIN

½ OZ. LUXARDO MARASCHINO LIQUEUR

¼ OZ. CRÈME DE VIOLETTE

½ OZ. FRESH LEMON JUICE

1 MARASCHINO CHERRY, FOR GARNISH

GLASSWARE: COCKTAIL GLASS

Aviation

A slightly longer shake than normal will serve you well with this one, as the additional dilution allows the numerous bold flavors to mesh.

1. Chill a cocktail glass in the freezer.

2. Place the gin, Luxardo, crème de violette, and lemon juice in a cocktail shaker, fill it two-thirds of the way with ice, and shake until chilled.

3. Strain into the chilled glass and garnish with the cherry.

Hanky Panky

This drink was created for the legendary actor and cocktail connoisseur Sir Charles Hawtrey, who needed a pick-him-up after a hard day. After trying it, he exclaimed: "By Jove, that is the real hanky-panky!" The name stuck.

1. Chill a cocktail glass in the freezer.

2. Place the gin, vermouth, and Fernet-Branca in a cocktail shaker, fill it two-thirds of the way with ice, and shake until chilled.

3. Strain into the chilled glass and garnish with the orange twist.

1½ OZ. GIN

1½ OZ. SWEET VERMOUTH

2 DASHES OF FERNET-BRANCA

1 ORANGE TWIST, FOR GARNISH

**GLASSWARE:
COCKTAIL GLASS**

2 OZ. LONDON DRY GIN

....

¾ OZ. FRESH LEMON JUICE

....

¾ OZ. HONEY SYRUP (SEE PAGE 30)

....

1 LEMON TWIST, FOR GARNISH

....

GLASSWARE:
ROCKS GLASS

Bee's Knees

If you're looking for a little more out of this one, try swapping in fresh orange juice for some portion of the lemon juice.

1. Place the gin, lemon juice, and syrup in a cocktail shaker, fill it two-thirds of the way with ice, and shake until chilled.

2. Strain over ice into a rocks glass and garnish with the lemon twist.

French 75

Some will insist that confectioners' sugar must serve as the sweetener in a French 75, so make sure you experiment before settling on your definitive version.

1. Place the sugar cube in a champagne flute and add the lemon juice.

2. Add the gin and top with the Champagne.

3. Garnish the cocktail with the lemon twist. Skewer the cherry with a toothpick and place it over the mouth of the champagne flute.

1 SUGAR CUBE

JUICE OF 1 LEMON WEDGE

1 OZ. GIN

2 OZ. CHAMPAGNE

1 LEMON TWIST, 1 MARASCHINO CHERRY, FOR GARNISH

GLASSWARE:
CHAMPAGNE FLUTE

1½ OZ. GIN

½ OZ. FRESH LIME JUICE

1 LIME TWIST, FOR GARNISH

GLASSWARE:
COCKTAIL GLASS

Gimlet

Most cocktail books will tell you to stir a Gimlet, but shaking it gives this standard a facelift.

1. Place the gin and lime juice in a cocktail shaker, fill it two-thirds of the way with ice, and shake until chilled.

2. Strain into a cocktail glass and garnish with the lime twist.

The Elder Fashion

See why St-Germain is also known as "bartender's ketchup," due to its ability to consistently shine in cocktails.

1. Place the gin, St-Germain, and bitters in a mixing glass, fill it two-thirds of the way with ice, and stir until chilled.

2. Strain over ice into a rocks glass and garnish with the slice of cucumber.

2 OZ. LONDON DRY GIN

½ OZ. ST-GERMAIN

DASH OF ORANGE BITTERS

1 CUCUMBER SLICE, FOR GARNISH

GLASSWARE:
ROCKS GLASS

1½ OZ. GIN

⅓ OZ. AVERNA AMARO

1 OZ. FRESH BLOOD ORANGE JUICE

GLASSWARE:
TUMBLER

My Faraway One

Just a little Averna Amaro goes a long way in adding to the depth of flavor in a cocktail.

1. Chill a tumbler in the freezer.

2. Place all of the ingredients in a cocktail shaker, fill it two-thirds of the way with ice, and shake until chilled.

3. Strain into the chilled glass.

This Kitchen Is for Dancing

Any time a cocktail can unite strong flavors like gin, orange juice, and Sambuca, you can be confident a good time awaits.

1. Chill a cocktail glass in the freezer.

2. Place all of the ingredients in a cocktail shaker, fill it two-thirds of the way with ice, and shake until chilled.

3. Strain into the chilled cocktail glass.

1 OZ. GIN

1 OZ. FRESH ORANGE JUICE

½ OZ. SAMBUCA

½ OZ. DRY VERMOUTH

GLASSWARE:
COCKTAIL GLASS

1½ OZ. GIN

2 TO 3 DASHES OF ANGOSTURA
BITTERS

1 STRIP OF LEMON PEEL

PINCH OF LEMON ZEST,
FOR GARNISH

GLASSWARE:
ROCKS GLASS

Pink Gin

Not much to this one, but the clean flavor and
sunset hues remind you of the value of keeping
things simple.

1. Place the gin and bitters in a rocks glass
    filled with ice and stir until chilled.

2. Express the strip of lemon peel over the
    cocktail and garnish with the pinch of lemon
    zest.

Maiden's Prayer

The apple juice helps draw out the famed fruitiness of Lillet even more, allowing it to stand toe-to-toe with gin.

1. Place the ingredients in a cocktail shaker, fill it two-thirds of the way with ice, and shake until chilled.

2. Strain into a rocks glass.

1 OZ. GIN

1 OZ. LILLET

1 OZ. APPLE JUICE

GLASSWARE:
ROCKS GLASS

2 OZ. GIN

4 OZ. GRAPEFRUIT JUICE

1 SPRIG OF ROSEMARY, 1 GRAPEFRUIT TWIST, FOR GARNISH

GLASSWARE:
HIGHBALL GLASS

Greyhound

Some will expect to find vodka in this drink, so make sure you check with anyone who signals a desire for one before whipping it up.

1. Fill a highball glass with ice, add the gin and grapefruit juice, and stir until chilled.

2. Garnish with the sprig of rosemary and the grapefruit twist.

Singapore Express

A much-simplified take on the Singapore Sling that manages to capture all of that drink's charm.

1. Place the gin, Cherry Heering, orange liqueur, and pineapple juice in a cocktail shaker, fill it two-thirds of the way with ice, and shake until chilled.

2. Strain over ice into a highball glass and garnish with the maraschino cherry and orange slice.

2 OZ. GIN

1 OZ. CHERRY HEERING

1 OZ. ORANGE LIQUEUR

3 OZ. PINEAPPLE JUICE

1 MARASCHINO CHERRY, 1 ORANGE SLICE, FOR GARNISH

GLASSWARE: HIGHBALL GLASS

3 OZ. GIN

¾ OZ. DRY VERMOUTH

SPLASH OF OLIVE BRINE

**3 PIMENTO-STUFFED OLIVES,
FOR GARNISH**

**GLASSWARE:
COCKTAIL GLASS**

Dirty Martini

Swapping blue-cheese stuffed olives in for the garnish is a much-loved variation among Martini devotees.

1. Place the gin, vermouth, and olive brine in a mixing glass, fill it two-thirds of the way with ice, and stir until chilled.

2. Strain into a cocktail glass and garnish with the olives skewered on a toothpick.

The Martinez

This drink, rumored to be the inspiration for the Martini, is commonly made with the far-more widespread London Dry gin, but it's worth seeking out Old Tom.

1. Place the gin, vermouth, Luxardo, and bitters in a mixing glass, fill it two-thirds of the way with ice, and stir until chilled.

2. Strain into a cocktail glass and garnish with the orange twist.

2 OZ. OLD TIM GIN

⅔ OZ. SWEET VERMOUTH

⅔ OZ. LUXARDO MARASCHINO LIQUEUR

DASH OF ANGOSTURA BITTERS

1 ORANGE TWIST, FOR GARNISH

GLASSWARE: COCKTAIL GLASS

1½ OZ. GIN

2 TEASPOONS DRY VERMOUTH

5 DROPS OF GRAND MARNIER

GLASSWARE:
COCKTAIL GLASS

Hondo

As you might expect, the Grand Marnier adds a touch of class to this straightforward serve.

1. Chill a cocktail glass in the freezer.

2. Place all of the ingredients in a mixing glass, fill it two-thirds of the way with ice, and stir until chilled.

3. Strain into the chilled glass.

Joy Division

Simple and complex, solemn and uplifting, just like its namesake.

1. Place the gin, vermouth, liqueur, and absinthe in a mixing glass, fill it two-thirds of the way with ice, and stir until chilled.

2. Strain into a coupe and garnish with the lemon twist.

2 OZ. LONDON DRY GIN

1 OZ. DRY VERMOUTH

½ OZ. TRIPLE SEC

3 DASHES OF ABSINTHE

1 LEMON TWIST, FOR GARNISH

GLASSWARE:
COUPE

1½ OZ. LONDON DRY GIN

½ OZ. SWEET VERMOUTH

½ OZ. DRY VERMOUTH

1 OZ. FRESH ORANGE JUICE

GLASSWARE:
COCKTAIL GLASS

Bronx

Should you find this a bit too dry for your liking, try increasing the sweet vermouth until you land in a place you like.

1. Chill a cocktail glass in the freezer.

2. Place all of the ingredients in a cocktail shaker, fill it two-thirds of the way with ice, and shake until chilled.

3. Double-strain into the chilled glass.

Gentleman Caller

More delicate than Campari, the aperitivo it resembles, Aperol is a wonderful addition to any home bar.

1. Place the gin, sherry, and Aperol in a mixing glass, fill it two-thirds of the way with ice, and stir until chilled.

2. Strain into a Nick & Nora glass and garnish with the strip of lemon peel.

1 OZ. GIN

1 OZ. FINO SHERRY

½ OZ. APEROL

1 STRIP OF LEMON PEEL, FOR GARNISH

GLASSWARE:
NICK & NORA GLASS

¾ OZ. LONDON DRY GIN

¾ OZ. BARROW'S INTENSE GINGER
LIQUEUR

¾ OZ. FRESH LEMON JUICE

¼ OZ. HONEY SYRUP (SEE PAGE 30)

1 LEMON WEDGE, FOR GARNISH

GLASSWARE:
COLLINS GLASS

Docile Cobra

The fiery flavor of Barrow's sparks this riff on the Bee's Knees.

1. Place the gin, liqueur, lemon juice, and honey syrup in a cocktail shaker, fill it two-thirds of the way with ice, and shake until chilled.

2. Pour the contents of the shaker into a Collins glass and garnish with the lemon wedge.

Alone in Kyoto

A good one for those quiet days when you just don't know who you're supposed to be.

1. Place the gin, lemon juice, and syrup in a cocktail shaker, fill it two-thirds of the way with ice, and shake until chilled.

2. Strain into a champagne flute, top with the Champagne, and garnish with the lemon twist.

1 OZ. OLD TOM GIN

½ OZ. FRESH LEMON JUICE

½ OZ. SIMPLE SYRUP (SEE PAGE30)

CHAMPAGNE, TO TOP

1 LEMON TWIST, FOR GARNISH

GLASSWARE:
CHAMPAGNE FLUTE

1½ OZ. GIN

½ OZ. FRESH LEMON JUICE

2 DASHES OF CRÈME DE VIOLETTE

½ OZ. LUXARDO MARASCHINO
LIQUEUR

GLASSWARE:
COCKTAIL GLASS

Purple Rain

Don't trust anyone who turns their nose up at
Prince, or this homage to the man.

1. Chill a cocktail glass in the freezer.

2. Place all of the ingredients in a cocktail
   shaker, fill it two-thirds of the way with ice,
   and shake until chilled.

3. Strain into the chilled glass.

White Negroni

Fans of Suze will swoon for this cocktail, as its bittersweet flavor and the icy backbone provided by the gin make it an ideal summer serve.

1. Place the gin, Suze, and Lillet in a mixing glass, fill it two-thirds of the way with ice, and stir until chilled.

2. Strain over an ice sphere into a rocks glass and garnish with the grapefruit twist.

1 OZ. LONDON DRY GIN

1 OZ. SUZE

1 OZ. LILLET

1 GRAPEFRUIT TWIST, FOR GARNISH

GLASSWARE: ROCKS GLASS

12 FRESH BASIL LEAVES

2 OZ. GIN

¾ OZ. FRESH LIME JUICE

⅓ OZ. SIMPLE SYRUP
(SEE PAGE 30)

1 SPRIG OF FRESH BASIL,
FOR GARNISH

GLASSWARE:
ROCKS GLASS

Gin Basil Smash

Originally named the Gin Pesto, this refreshing, aromatic wonder swept around the globe shortly after Jörg Meyer created it at Paris' Le Lion in 2008.

1. Place the basil leaves in a cocktail shaker and muddle. Add the gin, lime juice, and syrup, fill the shaker two-thirds of the way with ice, and shake until chilled.

2. Double-strain over ice into a rocks glass and garnish with the sprig of basil.

Breakfast Martini

Rise and shine with this classic.

1. Place the gin, Cointreau, and lemon juice in a cocktail shaker, fill it two-thirds of the way with ice, and shake until chilled.

2. Strain into a cocktail glass and garnish with the orange twist.

1¾ OZ. GIN

½ OZ. COINTREAU

½ OZ. FRESH LEMON JUICE

1 ORANGE TWIST, FOR GARNISH

GLASSWARE:
COCKTAIL GLASS

12 BLUEBERRIES

2 OZ. GIN

½ OZ. FRESH LEMON JUICE

1 OZ. CLUB SODA

1 LEMON WHEEL, FOR GARNISH

GLASSWARE:
ROCKS GLASS

Blueberry Sparkler

Gin's compatibility with fresh, sweet fruits is beautifully showcased in this refreshing cocktail.

1. Place the blueberries in a cocktail shaker and muddle. Add the gin and lemon juice, fill the shaker two-thirds of the way with ice, and shake until chilled.

2. Double-strain over ice into a rocks glass, top with the club soda, and garnish with the lemon wheel.

Gin Blossom

A fun spin on the Tom Collins, with orange liqueur providing the tartness and grenadine the sweetness.

1. Add the gin and liqueur to a rocks glass filled with ice.

2. Add the club soda and stir until chilled.

3. Add the grenadine, let it filter down into the cocktail, and garnish with the orange twist.

1½ OZ. GIN

1½ OZ. ORANGE LIQUEUR

3 OZ. CLUB SODA

SPLASH OF GRENADINE

1 ORANGE TWIST, FOR GARNISH

GLASSWARE:
ROCKS GLASS

2 OZ. GIN

2 OZ. CRANBERRY JUICE

SPLASH OF ORANGE LIQUEUR

½ OZ. FRESH LIME JUICE

1 LIME WHEEL, FOR GARNISH

GLASSWARE:
ROCKS GLASS

Gin & Juice

See why Snoop Dogg made such a fuss about this amalgam in one of his many mid-90s anthems.

1. Place the gin, cranberry juice, liqueur, and lime juice in a cocktail shaker, fill it two-thirds of the way with ice, and shake until chilled.

2. Strain over ice into a rocks glass and garnish with the lime wheel.

Ruby Fizz

By adding a bit of effervescence and sweetness to a Greyhound, you can brighten the darkest days.

1. Fill a highball glass with ice, add the gin and grapefruit juice, and stir to combine.

2. Add the club soda, stir until chilled, and top with the grenadine.

3. Garnish with the grapefruit wedge.

2 OZ. GIN

2 OZ. GRAPEFRUIT JUICE

2 OZ. CLUB SODA

SPLASH OF GRENADINE

1 GRAPEFRUIT WEDGE, FOR GARNISH

GLASSWARE:
HIGHBALL GLASS

SALT, FOR THE RIM

2 OZ. GIN

2 OZ. GRAPEFRUIT JUICE

2 OZ. CRANBERRY JUICE

1 GRAPEFRUIT WEDGE,
FOR GARNISH

GLASSWARE:
ROCKS GLASS

Salty Mutt

The salt is not there for decoration—as in food, it helps enhance all of the ingredients.

1. Rim a rocks glass with salt and then fill the glass with ice.

2. Place the gin, grapefruit juice, and cranberry juice in a cocktail shaker, fill it two-thirds of the way with ice, and shake until chilled.

3. Strain into the rimmed glass and garnish with the grapefruit wedge.

Snow Bowl

This beautiful, creamy cocktail was made to star at your holiday party.

1. Place the gin, liqueur, and crème de menthe in a cocktail shaker, fill it two-thirds of the way with ice, and shake until chilled.

2. Strain over ice into a rocks glass and garnish the cocktail with the dusting of nutmeg.

2 OZ. GIN

2 OZ. WHITE CHOCOLATE LIQUEUR

SPLASH OF WHITE CRÈME DE MENTHE

DUSTING OF FRESHLY GRATED NUTMEG, FOR GARNISH

GLASSWARE: ROCKS GLASS

Tequila & Mezcal

SALT, FOR THE RIM

• • • • • • • • • • • • • • • • • • • •

2 OZ. TEQUILA

• • • • • • • • • • • • • • • • • • • •

1 OZ. ORANGE LIQUEUR

• • • • • • • • • • • • • • • • • • • •

1 OZ. FRESH LIME JUICE

• • • • • • • • • • • • • • • • • • • •

1 LIME WHEEL, FOR GARNISH

• • • • • • • • • • • • • • • • • • • •

GLASSWARE:
COUPE

Margarita

While much debate rages over who came up with this drink, its pleasant taste and unquestioned status as the signal that it's time to let the good times roll have made it the most popular cocktail in America.

1. Rim a coupe with the salt and, if desired, add ice to the glass.

2. Place the tequila, triple sec, and lime juice in a cocktail shaker, fill it two-thirds of the way with ice, and shake until chilled.

3. Strain the cocktail into the glass and garnish with the lime wheel.

Paloma

Spanish for "dove," the Paloma provides a fitting clemency to any proceeding thanks to the always-in-step pairing of grapefruit and tequila.

1. Add the tequila, grapefruit juice, and lime juice to a highball glass filled with ice and stir until chilled.

2. Top with the grapefruit soda, gently stir, and garnish with the grapefruit wedge.

2 OZ. TEQUILA

1 OZ. GRAPEFRUIT JUICE

½ OZ. FRESH LIME JUICE

PINK GRAPEFRUIT SODA, TO TOP

1 GRAPEFRUIT WEDGE, FOR GARNISH

GLASSWARE:
HIGHBALL GLASS

1½ OZ. REPOSADO TEQUILA

½ OZ. MEZCAL

2 DASHES OF ANGOSTURA BITTERS

1 BAR SPOON AGAVE NECTAR

1 STRIP OF ORANGE PEEL, FOR GARNISH

GLASSWARE:
ROCKS GLASS

Oaxaca Old Fashioned

Created by agave spirits evangelist Phil Ward at the infamous Death & Co., this is the cocktail that pushed mezcal onto the American spirits scene.

1. Place the tequila, mezcal, bitters, and agave nectar in a rocks glass containing one large ice cube and stir until chilled.

2. Hold the strip of orange peel about 2 inches above a lit match for a couple of seconds. Twist and squeeze the peel over the lit match, while holding it above the cocktail and taking care to avoid the flames. If desired, rub the torched peel around the rim of the glass and then drop it into the drink.

TIP

Don't be afraid to experiment with the type of bitters employed in this one—in an evolved version Ward went with Bittermens Xocalatl Mole Bitters—or to go all-in on a mezcal-only version.

Cantaritos

In Jalisco, Mexico, this drink would be mixed and imbibed in a charming clay pot like the one in the photo. A Cantaritos is so refreshing that this delightful touch isn't essential, but it can't be argued that a Collins glass carries the same charm.

1. Add the tequila and juices to a Collins glass filled with ice and stir until chilled.

2. Top with the soda and garnish with the lime wedge.

2 OZ. REPOSADO TEQUILA

1½ OZ. FRESH ORANGE JUICE

¾ OZ. FRESH PINK GRAPEFRUIT JUICE

2 OZ. PINK GRAPEFRUIT SODA

1 LIME WEDGE, FOR GARNISH

GLASSWARE:
COLLINS GLASS

¾ OZ. MEZCAL

¾ OZ. YELLOW CHARTREUSE

¾ OZ. APEROL

¾ OZ. FRESH LIME JUICE

GLASSWARE:
COUPE

Naked & Famous

The salmon pink color is a bit deceptive, as the drink is smoky thanks to the mezcal and bittersweet thanks to the Aperol.

1. Chill a coupe in the freezer.

2. Place all of the ingredients in a cocktail shaker, fill the shaker two-thirds of the way with ice, and shake until chilled.

3. Strain into the chilled coupe.

Tequila Sunrise

Regardless of your feelings on the Eagles, a few of these enjoyed in good company will help you understand their need to immortalize this cocktail with an ode.

1. Add the tequila and juices to a highball glass filled with ice and stir until chilled.

2. Add the grenadine and do not stir, letting it filter down through the orange juice.

3. Garnish with the maraschino cherry and orange slice.

2 OZ. TEQUILA

DASH OF LEMON JUICE

4 OZ. ORANGE JUICE

SPLASH OF GRENADINE

1 MARASCHINO CHERRY, 1 ORANGE
SLICE, FOR GARNISH

GLASSWARE:
HIGHBALL GLASS

1 OZ. TEQUILA

1 OZ. GRAPEFRUIT SODA

2 OZ. CHAMPAGNE

**GLASSWARE:
CHAMPAGNE FLUTE**

Unlikely Allies

Cutting the slight sweetness of the soda with the dry Champagne allows every flavor to shine its brightest.

1. Place the tequila and soda in a champagne flute and gently swirl to combine.

2. Top with the Champagne.

Blooming Cactus

If you're blood's boiling following a tough day, this one's as cool as a desert evening.

1. Place the mint leaves and lime juice in a cocktail shaker and muddle.

2. Add ice along with the tequila and cranberry juice and shake until chilled.

3. Strain into a mason jar filled with ice and garnish with the lime wheel.

6 FRESH MINT LEAVES, TORN

DASH OF LIME JUICE

1 OZ. TEQUILA

4 OZ. CRANBERRY JUICE

1 LIME WHEEL, FOR GARNISH

GLASSWARE:
MASON JAR

2 OZ. TEQUILA

SPLASH OF ORANGE LIQUEUR

¼ OZ. FRESH LIME JUICE

4 OZ. GINGER BEER

1 LIME WHEEL, FOR GARNISH

GLASSWARE:
COPPER MUG

The Burro

Swapping tequila in for the vodka carries the Moscow Mule to unprecedented heights.

1. Add the tequila, triple sec, and lime juice to a copper mug filled with ice and stir to combine.

2. Top with the ginger beer and garnish with the lime wheel.

Baja Lemonade

The rosemary ties everything together in this refreshing serve.

1. Place the rosemary, tequila, and coconut rum in a cocktail shaker, fill it two-thirds of the way with ice, and shake until chilled.

2. Strain over ice into a tumbler, top with the lemonade, and garnish with the lemon wheel.

1 SPRIG OF FRESH ROSEMARY

2 OZ. TEQUILA

SPLASH OF COCONUT RUM

4 OZ. LEMONADE

1 LEMON WHEEL, FOR GARNISH

**GLASSWARE:
TUMBLER**

½ OZ. SIMPLE SYRUP
(SEE PAGE 30)

3 DASHES OF ORANGE BITTERS

2 OZ. AÑEJO TEQUILA

1 STRIP OF LEMON PEEL,
FOR GARNISH

GLASSWARE:
ROCKS GLASS

What's New

A contemporary updating on a somewhat stodgy favorite.

1. Chill a rocks glass in the freezer.

2. Place the syrup, bitters, and tequila in the chilled rocks glass and stir to combine.

3. Add 2 large ice cubes to the glass and stir until chilled.

4. Garnish with the strip of lemon peel.

El Joven

Try this if you find a Margarita to be just a little too sweet.

1. Place the tequila and lime juice in a cocktail shaker, fill it two-thirds of the way with ice, and shake until chilled.

2. Strain over ice into a highball glass, top with the seltzer, and garnish with the lime wedge.

2 OZ. TEQUILA

1 OZ. FRESH LIME JUICE

SELTZER WATER, TO TOP

1 LIME WEDGE, FOR GARNISH

GLASSWARE:
HIGHBALL GLASS

1½ OZ. TEQUILA

1½ OZ. CHERRY HEERING

½ OZ. FRESH LIME JUICE

3 OZ. ORANGE JUICE

1 MARASCHINO CHERRY,
FOR GARNISH

GLASSWARE:
HIGHBALL GLASS

Early Night

This reworking of the Tequila Sunrise is so delicious you need to be careful about how quickly you take it down.

1. Add the tequila, cherry liqueur, and juices to a highball glass filled with ice and stir until chilled.

2. Garnish with the maraschino cherry.

The High Roller

Champagne is the chef's kiss to this top-shelf take on the Margarita.

1. Rim a rocks glass with the fleur de sel and add ice to the glass.

2. Place the tequila, Grand Marnier, and lime juice in a cocktail shaker, fill it two-thirds of the way with ice, and shake until chilled.

3. Strain into the rocks glass, top with the Champagne, and garnish with the lime twist.

FLEUR DE SEL, FOR THE RIM

2 OZ. PREMIUM TEQUILA

1 OZ. GRAND MARNIER

1 OZ. FRESH LIME JUICE

4 OZ. CHAMPAGNE

1 LIME TWIST, FOR GARNISH

GLASSWARE:
ROCKS GLASS

1½ OZ. TEQUILA

½ OZ. DRY VERMOUTH

½ OZ. TRIPLE SEC

SPLASH OF GRENADINE

1 ORANGE TWIST, FOR GARNISH

GLASSWARE:
ROCKS GLASS

Silverblood

Clear away all doubt with this sanguine-sounding cocktail.

1. Place the tequila, vermouth, triple sec, and grenadine in a cocktail shaker, fill it two-thirds of the way with ice, and shake until chilled.

2. Strain over ice into a rocks glass and garnish with the orange twist.

Coconut Margarita

If you don't want to make this into a frozen drink, simply add all of the ingredients to a cocktail shaker with ice and shake until chilled.

1. Rim a tumbler with the coconut shavings and add ice to the glass.

2. Place the tequila, coconut rum, and lime juice in a blender, add ½ cup ice, and puree until smooth.

3. Strain into the tumbler and garnish with the lime wheel.

SHREDDED COCONUT, FOR THE RIM

2 OZ. TEQUILA

1 OZ. COCONUT RUM

1 OZ. LIME JUICE

1 LIME WHEEL, FOR GARNISH

GLASSWARE:
TUMBLER

1 OZ. TEQUILA

1 OZ. CRÈME DE MURE

1 OZ. FRESH LIME JUICE

2 OZ. GINGER BEER

1 SAGE LEAF, FOR GARNISH

GLASSWARE:
DOUBLE ROCKS GLASS

Kinda Knew Anna

Don't mistake crème de mure as some exotic ingredient—it's simply blackberry liqueur.

1. Place the tequila, liqueur, and lime juice in a cocktail shaker, fill it two-thirds of the way with ice, and shake until chilled.

2. Strain over ice into a double rocks glass, top with the ginger beer, and garnish with the sage leaf.

El Diablo

Cutting against the sweetness of the liqueur with spicy ginger beer is what lends this cocktail the devilish touch suggested by the name.

1. Place the tequila, crème de cassis, and lime juice in a cocktail shaker, fill it two-thirds of the way with ice, and shake until chilled.

2. Strain over ice into a mason jar, top with ginger beer, garnish with the slice of lemon and a blackberry.

1½ OZ. TEQUILA

1 OZ. CRÈME DE CASSIS

1 OZ. FRESH LIME JUICE

GINGER BEER, TO TOP

1 LEMON SLICE, 1 BLACKBERRY, FOR GARNISH

GLASSWARE:
MASON JAR

1 OZ. TEQUILA

1 OZ. PISCO

¾ OZ. FRESH LIME JUICE

¾ OZ. SIMPLE SYRUP
(SEE PAGE 30)

3 DASHES OF ANGOSTURA
BITTERS, FOR GARNISH

**GLASSWARE:
TUMBLER**

Jalisco
Sour

Slipping a bit of tequila into a Pisco Sour adds
considerable depth to the beguiling classic.

1. Place the tequila, pisco, lime juice, and syrup
    in a cocktail shaker, fill it two-thirds of the
    way with crushed ice, and shake until chilled.

2. Strain into a tumbler and garnish with the
    bitters.

Ranch Water

The gentle bubbles and slight salinity of Topo Chico are key to this simple refresher.

1. Pour out 2 oz. of the Topo Chico and add the tequila and lime juice to the bottle.

2. Garnish with the lime wedge.

1 (12 OZ.) BOTTLE OF TOPO CHICO

1½ OZ. TEQUILA

¼ OZ. FRESH LIME JUICE

1 LIME WEDGE, FOR GARNISH

GLASSWARE:
BOTTLE OF TOPO CHICO

1¼ OZ. TEQUILA

2 OZ. PINEAPPLE JUICE

1 OZ. FRESH LIME JUICE

1 LIME WHEEL, FOR GARNISH

GLASSWARE:
COCKTAIL GLASS

Matador

Some versions of this drink include grenadine, so don't hesitate to add it if it isn't sweet enough for you.

1. Place the tequila, pineapple juice, and lime juice in a cocktail shaker, fill it two-thirds of the way with ice, and shake until chilled.

2. Strain into a cocktail glass and garnish with the lime wheel.

She's a Rainbow

If you remember Midori as being too sweet, you should try it again. Suntory has recently cut back the sugar content by 20 percent.

1. Place the tequila, Midori, and juice in a cocktail shaker, fill it two-thirds of the way with ice, and shake vigorously.

2. Strain over ice into a highball glass and garnish with the slice of grapefruit.

2 OZ. TEQUILA

1 OZ. MIDORI

5 OZ. WHITE GRAPEFRUIT JUICE

1 GRAPEFRUIT SLICE, FOR GARNISH

GLASSWARE:
HIGHBALL GLASS

½ OZ. HIBISCUS TEA SYRUP
(SEE PAGE 30)

¾ OZ. FRESH LEMON JUICE

¼ OZ. LUXARDO MARASCHINO
LIQUEUR

1½ OZ. MEZCAL

GLASSWARE:
NICK & NORA GLASS

Set It Off

The nutty, slightly smoky flavor of Luxardo was made to partner with mezcal.

1. Place the syrup, lemon juice, Luxardo, and tequila in a cocktail shaker, fill it two-thirds of the way with ice, and shake until chilled.

2. Strain into a Nick & Nora glass.

True Romance

Fresh, zesty, and bittersweet, this one is love at first sight.

1. Place the mezcal, Chartreuse, and amaro in a rocks glass containing one large ice cube and stir until chilled.

2. Garnish with the lime twist and the pinch of sea salt.

1½ OZ. MEZCAL

1 OZ. YELLOW CHARTREUSE

¾ OZ. AVERNA AMARO

1 LIME TWIST, PINCH OF SEA SALT, FOR GARNISH

GLASSWARE:
ROCKS GLASS

1 OZ. FRESHLY BREWED ESPRESSO

2 OZ. MEZCAL

½ OZ. CINNAMON SYRUP
(SEE PAGE 30)

1 STRIP OF ORANGE PEEL,
FOR GARNISH

GLASSWARE:
NICK & NORA GLASS

Cooper's Café

If you want this iced, top up your glass with Topo Chico.

1. Place the espresso, mezcal, and syrup in a cocktail shaker, fill it two-thirds of the way with ice, and shake until chilled.

2. Strain into a Nick & Nora glass and garnish with the strip of orange peel.

A Rainy Afternoon

This one's got no shortage of bite to it, making it perfect for any day that gets washed away.

1. Place the tequila, liqueur, and juices in a cocktail shaker, fill it two-thirds of the way with ice, and shake until chilled.

2. Strain over ice into a highball glass and garnish with the lime wheel.

2 OZ. TEQUILA

1 OZ. SOUR APPLE LIQUEUR

1 OZ. APPLE JUICE

1 OZ. FRESH LIME JUICE

1 LIME WHEEL, FOR GARNISH

GLASSWARE:
HIGHBALL GLASS

Vodka

1 OZ. VODKA

1 OZ. TRIPLE SEC

1½ OZ. CRANBERRY JUICE

½ OZ. FRESH LIME JUICE

1 LIME WHEEL, FOR GARNISH

GLASSWARE:
COCKTAIL GLASS

Cosmopolitan

Though it surged in popularity thanks to HBO's *Sex in the City*, this cocktail has the pedigree to continue standing tall after the buzz has faded away.

1. Chill a cocktail glass in the freezer.

2. Place the vodka, triple sec, cranberry juice, and lime juice in a cocktail shaker, fill it two-thirds of the way with ice, and shake until chilled.

3. Strain into the chilled cocktail glass and garnish with the lime wheel.

White Russian

As everyone knows, the Coen Brothers' late '90s masterwork, *The Big Lebowski*, breathed considerable life into this creamy cocktail, which had lost its way during the calorie-conscious '80s.

1. Place a few ice cubes in a rocks glass.

2. Add the vodka and Kahlúa and stir until chilled. Top with a generous splash of heavy cream and slowly stir until combined.

2 OZ. VODKA

1 OZ. KAHLÚA

HEAVY CREAM, TO TASTE

GLASSWARE:
ROCKS GLASS

4 FRESH MINT LEAVES

JUICE OF ½ LIME

2 OZ. VODKA

6 OZ. GINGER BEER

1 LIME WEDGE, FOR GARNISH

GLASSWARE:
COPPER MUG

Moscow Mule

If you'd like, you can use the mint leaves as a garnish and add a dash of simple syrup.

1. Place the mint leaves at the bottom of a copper mug, add the lime juice, and muddle.

2. Add crushed ice to the mug, add the vodka and ginger beer, and garnish with the lime wedge.

Mudslide

It remains the height of decadent and delicious dessert drinks.

1. Place the vodka, liqueurs, and ice cream in a blender, add ½ cup ice, and puree to desired consistency.

2. Pour the cocktail into a Daiquiri glass and garnish with a dusting of cocoa powder.

1½ OZ. VODKA

1½ OZ. KAHLÚA

1½ OZ. CREAM LIQUEUR

¾ CUP VANILLA ICE CREAM

COCOA POWDER, FOR GARNISH

GLASSWARE:
DAIQUIRI GLASS

3 OZ. GIN

1 OZ. VODKA

½ OZ. LILLET BLANC OR COCCHI
AMERICANO

1 LEMON TWIST, FOR GARNISH

GLASSWARE:
COUPE

Vesper Martini

The Vesper Martini was born on the pages of Ian Fleming's 1953 book *Casino Royale*, with James Bond delivering strict instructions for his peculiar order. Because the Kina Lillet that Bond requested no longer exists, Lillet Blanc or Cocchi Americano must serve in its stead.

1. Chill a coupe in the freezer.

2. Add the gin, vodka, and Lillet or Cocchi Americano to a cocktail shaker, fill it two-thirds of the way with ice, and shake until chilled.

3. Strain into the chilled coupe and garnish with the lemon twist.

Espresso Martini

Even if it will cool in the shaker, be sure to use a steaming hot shot of espresso so that the cocktail retains the crema.

1. Chill a cocktail glass in the freezer.

2. Place the vodka, espresso, and Kahlúa in a cocktail shaker, fill it two-thirds of the way with ice, and shake until chilled.

3. Double-strain into the chilled glass and garnish with the three espresso beans.

2 OZ. VODKA

1 OZ. FRESHLY BREWED ESPRESSO

½ OZ. KAHLÚA

3 ESPRESSO BEANS, FOR GARNISH

GLASSWARE:
COCKTAIL GLASS

3 OZ. VODKA

1 OZ. DRY VERMOUTH

SPLASH OF GREEN OLIVE BRINE

PIMENTO-STUFFED GREEN OLIVES,
FOR GARNISH

GLASSWARE:
COCKTAIL GLASS

The Dirty Spy

For many people, a Martini contains gin, not vodka, but that doesn't mean this variation isn't wonderful in its own right.

1. Place the vodka, vermouth, and olive brine in a cocktail shaker, fill it two-thirds of the way with ice, and shake until chilled.

2. Strain into a cocktail glass and garnish with the olives.

Screwdriver

Vodka and any juice can work as a cocktail, but none will work as well as vodka and orange juice.

1. Fill a highball glass with ice, add the vodka, and top with the orange juice.

2. Stir until chilled and garnish with the orange slice.

2 OZ. VODKA

4 OZ. ORANGE JUICE

1 ORANGE SLICE, FOR GARNISH

GLASSWARE:
HIGHBALL GLASS

1¼ OZ. VODKA

3 OZ. FRESH ORANGE JUICE

½ OZ. GALLIANO

1 ORANGE SLICE, FOR GARNISH

GLASSWARE:
HIGHBALL GLASS

Harvey Wallbanger

Fresh orange juice is the key to restoring this cocktail to the glory of its '70s heyday.

1. Add the orange juice and vodka to a highball glass with ice and stir until chilled.

2. Float the Galliano on top by pouring it over the back of a spoon and garnish with the orange slice.

Essential Bloody Mary

As you likely know, this cocktail can be taken in a number of directions, but this is all you need to achieve its fabled restorative deliciousness.

1. Add the Worcestershire sauce, lemon juice, vodka, and tomato juice to a highball glass containing ice and stir until chilled.

2. Garnish with anything your heart desires. Celery, olives, bacon, lemon wedges, and pickles are popular options.

DASH OF WORCESTERSHIRE SAUCE

DASH OF FRESH LEMON JUICE

2 OZ. VODKA

4 OZ. TOMATO JUICE

GARNISH WITH ANYTHING YOUR HEART DESIRES

GLASSWARE:
HIGHBALL GLASS

1½ OZ. VODKA

1½ OZ. PEACH SCHNAPPS

4 OZ. ORANGE JUICE

SPLASH OF PINEAPPLE JUICE

1 ORANGE SLICE, FOR GARNISH

GLASSWARE:
HIGHBALL GLASS

Hairy Navel

Adding vodka and pineapple juice to the infamous Fuzzy Navel dries out the proceedings enough that even cocktail snobs won't mind imbibing.

1. Fill a highball glass with ice, add the vodka, schnapps, and orange juice, and stir until chilled.

2. Top with a splash of pineapple juice and garnish with the orange slice.

Blue Lagoon

Yes, it's as refreshing as it looks in the glass.

1. Place the vodka and blue Curaçao in a cocktail shaker, fill it two-thirds of the way with ice, and shake until chilled.

2. Strain over ice into a mason jar and top with the lemonade and lime juice. Gently stir to combine.

3. Garnish with the slice of lemon and maraschino cherry.

1½ OZ. VODKA

1½ OZ. BLUE CURAÇAO

6 OZ. LEMONADE

DASH OF LIME JUICE

1 LEMON SLICE, 1 MARASCHINO CHERRY, FOR GARNISH

GLASSWARE:
MASON JAR

2 OZ. VODKA

SPLASH OF TRIPLE SEC

2 OZ. GRAPEFRUIT JUICE

4 OZ. GINGER ALE

1 LIME WHEEL, FOR GARNISH

GLASSWARE:
TUMBLER

Feel Flows

A bit of spice and sweetness from the ginger ale ties everything together beautifully here.

1. Fill a tumbler with ice and add the vodka, triple sec, and grapefruit juice.

2. Stir until chilled, top with the ginger ale, and gently stir to combine.

3. Garnish with the lime wheel.

The Pickle Kid

An homage to the legendary late-night duo of Hoss & Bronco.

1. Place the vodka, vermouth, and pickle juice in a mixing glass, fill it two-thirds of the way with ice, and stir until chilled.

2. Strain into a cocktail glass and garnish with the pickle chips.

3 OZ. VODKA

¾ OZ. DRY VERMOUTH

SPLASH OF PICKLE JUICE

1 PICKLE CHIP, FOR GARNISH

GLASSWARE:
COCKTAIL GLASS

SUGAR, FOR THE RIM

·······································

2 OZ. VODKA

·······································

1 OZ. TRIPLE SEC

·······································

1 OZ. FRESH LEMON JUICE

·······································

1 LEMON TWIST, FOR GARNISH

·······································

GLASSWARE:
COCKTAIL GLASS

Lemon Drop

You may be familiar with this as a shot, but it's just as delicious in its grown-up form.

1. Wet the rim of a cocktail glass and rim it with the sugar.

2. Place the vodka, triple sec, and lemon juice in a cocktail shaker, fill it two-thirds of the way with ice, and shake until chilled.

3. Strain the cocktail into the rimmed glass and garnish with the lemon twist.

Pray Up, Stay Up

The hint of almond that has earned Heering so many loyal fans gets a chance to recruit many more in this drink.

1. Chill a cocktail glass in the freezer.

2. Place all of the ingredients in a mixing glass, fill it two-thirds of the way with ice, and stir until chilled.

3. Strain the cocktail into the chilled glass.

1¾ OZ. VODKA

½ OZ. CHERRY HEERING

4 DROPS OF COINTREAU

3 TO 4 DROPS OF ANGOSTURA BITTERS

GLASSWARE:
COCKTAIL GLASS

½ OZ. DARK CHOCOLATE LIQUEUR

¾ OZ. KAHLÚA

1¼ OZ. STOLICHNAYA HOT VODKA
(OR ANY SPICY VODKA)

¾ OZ. ISLAY SCOTCH WHISKY

GLASSWARE:
COCKTAIL GLASS

No Way Back

People who sneer at vodka-based cocktails will be floored by the bold flavors available here.

1. Place all of the ingredients in a mixing glass, fill it two-thirds of the way with ice, and stir until chilled.

2. Strain into a cocktail glass.

Dr. Funk

Quality is always important in cocktail making, but that's especially the case when using flavored vodkas, as the lower-end offerings can easily sink a drink. For this one, Ciroc Peach is a good bet to supply the desired result.

1. Add the vodka and cranberry juice to a mixing glass, fill it two-thirds of the way with ice, and stir until chilled.

2. Strain into a champagne flute, top with sparkling wine, and garnish with a lemon twist.

1 OZ. PEACH-FLAVORED VODKA

1 OZ. CRANBERRY JUICE

SPARKLING WINE, TO TOP

1 LEMON TWIST, FOR GARNISH

GLASSWARE:
CHAMPAGNE FLUTE

1½ OZ. VODKA

1½ OZ. JÄGERMEISTER

¾ OZ. FRESH LEMON JUICE

1 LEMON WHEEL, FOR GARNISH

GLASSWARE:
HIGHBALL GLASS

Great Idea

A drink that came together after experimenting with what little liquor was on hand, and ended up being a brilliant move.

1. Add the vodka, liqueur, and lemon juice to a highball glass and gently stir to combine.

2. Add ice to the glass and garnish the cocktail with the lemon wheel.

You Know, You Know

For fans of Topo Chico, this drink's ability to refresh will come as no surprise.

1. Wet the rim of a highball glass and rim it with salt.

2. Add ice to the glass along with the vodka and lemon juice. Top with the Topo Chico and stir until chilled.

3. Garnish with the lemon wheel.

SALT, FOR THE RIM

1½ OZ. VODKA

2 OZ. FRESH LEMON JUICE

TOPO CHICO, TO TOP

1 LEMON WHEEL, FOR GARNISH

GLASSWARE:
HIGHBALL GLASS

2 OZ. BLUEBERRY-FLAVORED VODKA

1 OZ. SIMPLE SYRUP (SEE PAGE 30)

1 OZ. FRESH LEMON JUICE

GLASSWARE:
ROCKS GLASS

Sweet Juju

Western Son, a Texas distillery, is the brand you'll want to center your search for blueberry vodka around.

1. Place all of the ingredients in a cocktail shaker, fill it two-thirds of the way with ice, and shake until chilled.

2. Strain over ice into a rocks glass.

Seabreeze

Some recipes will include fresh lime juice, so give that a try if you're looking for a little something more from this drink. Shaking the ingredients instead of simply building the cocktail in the glass has also found favor with some folks.

1. Add the vodka, cranberry juice, and grapefruit juice to a highball glass containing ice.

2. Stir until chilled and garnish with the slice of grapefruit.

2 OZ. VODKA

4 OZ. CRANBERRY JUICE

2 OZ. GRAPEFRUIT JUICE

1 GRAPEFRUIT SLICE, FOR GARNISH

GLASSWARE:
HIGHBALL GLASS

2 OZ. VANILLA VODKA

2 OZ. PEAR NECTAR

SPLASH OF FRESH LIME JUICE

1 PEAR SLICE, FOR GARNISH

GLASSWARE:
ROCKS GLASS

Pear Pressure

Highlighting the flavored vodka with the subtle vanilla notes present in pears makes this a winner.

1. Place the vodka, nectar, and lime juice in a cocktail shaker, fill it two-thirds of the way with ice, and shake until chilled.

2. Strain over ice into a rocks glass and garnish with the slice of pear.

My Silks and Fine Array

Much like the Julie Covington song that lent its name to this drink, this is an underappreciated gem.

1. Add all of the ingredients to a cocktail shaker, fill it two-thirds of the way with ice, and shake until chilled.

2. Strain over ice into a rocks glass.

1 OZ. VODKA

1 OZ. CHOCOLATE LIQUEUR

1 OZ. KAHLÚA

2 OZ. MILK

GLASSWARE:
ROCKS GLASS

2 OZ. VODKA

1 OZ. SOUR APPLE LIQUEUR

½ OZ. FRESH LIME JUICE

⅓ OZ. SIMPLE SYRUP
(SEE PAGE 30)

1 THIN APPLE SLICE, FOR GARNISH

GLASSWARE:
COCKTAIL GLASS

Appletini

See why this sour twist took over cocktail menus at the dawn of the new millennium.

1. Chill a cocktail glass in the freezer.

2. Place the vodka, liqueur, lime juice, and syrup in a cocktail shaker, fill it two-thirds of the way with ice, and shake until chilled.

3. Strain into the chilled glass and garnish with the apple slice.

Creamsicle

If you want to make this a frozen drink, use vanilla ice cream instead of the cream and blend with ½ cup ice.

1. Add the juice, vodka, cream, and triple sec to a mixing glass, fill it two-thirds of the way with ice, and stir until chilled.

2. Strain over ice into a rocks glass and garnish with the orange slice.

1½ OZ. ORANGE JUICE

1½ OZ. VODKA

1½ OZ. CREAM

SPLASH OF TRIPLE SEC

1 ORANGE SLICE, FOR GARNISH

GLASSWARE:
ROCKS GLASS

1½ OZ. CRANBERRY-FLAVORED
VODKA

3 OZ. LEMONADE

SPLASH OF FRESH LIME JUICE

1 LEMON TWIST, FOR GARNISH

GLASSWARE:
ROCKS GLASS

Summer
Splash

Finlandia's offering is the cranberry vodka you want to hold out for when considering this cocktail.

1. Add the vodka, lemonade, and lime juice to a cocktail shaker, fill it two-thirds of the way with ice, and shake until chilled.

2. Strain over ice into a rocks glass and garnish with the lemon twist.

Long Island Expressway

Not the boozy, all-hands-on-deck offering that the New York outpost is best known for, but it'll get you where you need to go.

1. Add the lemon juice, vodka, triple sec, and cola to a highball glass containing ice and stir until chilled.

2. Garnish with the lemon wheel.

½ OZ. FRESH LEMON JUICE

2 OZ. VODKA

SPLASH OF TRIPLE SEC

4 OZ. COLA

1 LEMON WHEEL, FOR GARNISH

GLASSWARE:
HIGHBALL GLASS

2 OZ. VODKA

6 OZ. GRAPEFRUIT JUICE

2 OZ. CLUB SODA

4 SPRIGS OF FRESH THYME

GLASSWARE:
COUPE

Borrowed Thyme

The duo of thyme and grapefruit sing a surprisingly sweet song.

1. Place the vodka, grapefruit juice, club soda, and 3 sprigs of the thyme in a mixing glass, fill it two-thirds of the way with ice, and stir until chilled.

2. Double-strain into a coupe and garnish with the remaining sprig of thyme.

Peach Tree Iced Tea

A piece of pure enjoyment that was made for summertime sipping.

1. Place the mint leaves and peach schnapps in a highball glass and muddle.

2. Add ice to the glass along with the vodka and iced tea. Stir until chilled.

6 FRESH MINT LEAVES, TORN

1½ OZ. PEACH SCHNAPPS

1½ OZ. VODKA

3 OZ. ICED TEA

GLASSWARE:
HIGHBALL GLASS

Rum

2 OZ. WHITE RUM

½ OZ. FRESH LIME JUICE

½ TEASPOON CASTER SUGAR

1 LIME WHEEL, FOR GARNISH

GLASSWARE:
COUPE

Daiquiri

A world away from the packaged, cloyingly sweet slush that many people know from the restaurant excursions of their youth and trips to the tropics. Its perfect balance of tart and sweet is beloved by bartenders everywhere.

1. Chill a coupe in the freezer.

2. Add the rum, lime juice, and caster sugar to a cocktail shaker, fill it two-thirds of the way with ice, and shake until chilled.

3. Strain into the chilled coupe and garnish with the lime wheel.

CASTER SUGAR

Caster sugar is a super-fine sugar with a consistency that sits somewhere between granulated sugar and confectioners' sugar. Since it can dissolve without heat, unlike granulated sugar, it is tailor-made for cocktails. This ideal fit comes with a hefty price tag at the store, but you can easily make caster sugar at home with nothing more than a food processor or a blender and some granulated sugar. Place the granulated sugar in the food processor or blender and pulse until the consistency is super-fine, but short of powdery. Let the sugar settle in the food processor or blender, transfer it to a container, and label it to avoid future confusion.

Mojito

It is rumored that the Mojito's name is derived from the West African word *mojo*, which means "to cast a little spell." As advertised, the refreshing character of a well-made Mojito is certain to put everyone who encounters it in a pleasant daze.

1. Place the mint leaves in the palm of one hand and slap them to activate their aroma. Place them in the bottom of a Collins glass and add the syrup and lime juice.

2. Fill the glass halfway with crushed ice. Gently stir until lightly chilled, about 10 seconds. Add the rum and more crushed ice and briefly stir to combine.

3. Fill the remainder of the glass with crushed ice and garnish with the sprig of mint.

8 TO 10 FRESH MINT LEAVES

1 OZ. SIMPLE SYRUP (SEE PAGE 30)

1 OZ. FRESH LIME JUICE

2 OZ. WHITE RUM

1 SPRIG OF FRESH MINT, FOR GARNISH

GLASSWARE: COLLINS GLASS

2 OZ. NAVY RUM (PUSSER'S RECOMMENDED)

1 OZ. CREAM OF COCONUT

1 OZ. ORANGE JUICE

4 OZ. PINEAPPLE JUICE

FRESHLY GRATED NUTMEG, 1 ORANGE SLICE, FOR GARNISH

GLASSWARE: MASON JAR

Painkiller

A considerable amount of fruity flavor masks the muscle of the overproof navy rum, allowing your every last ache to disappear without a trace.

1. Place the rum, cream of coconut, orange juice, and pineapple juice in a cocktail shaker, fill it two-thirds of the way with crushed ice, and shake until chilled.

2. Pour the contents of the shaker into a mason jar, grate nutmeg over the cocktail, and garnish with the orange slice.

Hemingway Daiquiri

Ernest Hemingway's impact on literature was immense, but it could be argued that his influence on cocktail culture was even larger. Featuring prominently in the history of the Bloody Mary, the Martini, and the Mojito, Hemingway also lends his name to the most popular variation on the Daiquiri.

1. Chill a coupe in the freezer.

2. Place the rum, grapefruit juice, lime juice, and Luxardo in a cocktail shaker, fill the shaker two-thirds of the way with ice, and shake until chilled.

3. Double-strain into the chilled coupe and garnish with the grapefruit twist.

2 OZ. WHITE RUM

¾ OZ. FRESH PINK GRAPEFRUIT JUICE

½ OZ. FRESH LIME JUICE

¼ OZ. LUXARDO MARASCHINO LIQUEUR

1 GRAPEFRUIT TWIST, FOR GARNISH

GLASSWARE:
COUPE

1½ OZ. BLACK RUM

½ OZ. CAMPARI

1½ OZ. PINEAPPLE JUICE

⅓ OZ. FRESH LIME JUICE

2 PINEAPPLE CHUNKS,
FOR GARNISH

GLASSWARE:
ROCKS GLASS

Jungle Bird

One of the few tiki classics that did not issue from the innovative mind of Don the Beachcomber.

1. Place the rum, Campari, and juices in a cocktail shaker, fill the shaker two-thirds of the way with ice, and shake until chilled.

2. Strain into a rocks glass filled with crushed ice and garnish with the pineapple chunks.

Caipirinha

Most bars in America will serve this cocktail over crushed ice, but utilizing water in the ingredients means you don't need any additional dilution.

1. Place the lime juice, syrup, and water in a mixing glass and stir to combine.

2. Add ice and the caçhaca and stir until chilled.

3. Strain into a Collins glass containing large ice cubes.

½ OZ. FRESH LIME JUICE

½ OZ. SIMPLE SYRUP
(SEE PAGE 30)

¾ OZ. WATER

2 OZ. CAÇHACA, CHILLED IN
FREEZER

GLASSWARE:
COLLINS GLASS

½ OZ. FRESH LIME JUICE

2 OZ. WHITE RUM

4 OZ. COLA

DASH OF ANGOSTURA BITTERS

1 LIME WEDGE, FOR GARNISH

GLASSWARE:
ROCKS GLASS

Cuba Libre

It bears much resemblance to many people's first drink, the Rum & Coke, but features far more complexity thanks to the lime juice and bitters.

1. Place the lime juice, rum, and cola in a Rocks glass filled with ice and stir until chilled.

2. Top with the bitters and garnish with the lime wedge.

Roses for Alex

Do something sweet for someone you love, and whip up a batch of these.

1. Add the rum, liqueur, and club soda to a rocks glass filled with ice and stir until chilled.

2. Add the splash of grenadine and garnish with the maraschino cherry.

1½ OZ. WHITE RUM

1½ OZ. ORANGE LIQUEUR

2 OZ. CLUB SODA

SPLASH OF GRENADINE

1 MARASCHINO CHERRY, FOR GARNISH

GLASSWARE: ROCKS GLASS

1 OZ. WHITE RUM

1 OZ. KAHLÚA

1 OZ. IRISH CREAM

DASH OF WHITE CRÈME
DE MENTHE

1 SPRIG OF FRESH MINT,
FOR GARNISH

GLASSWARE:
ROCKS GLASS

All the Hearts

Delicious and decadent, you'd be wise to save this one till after dinner.

1. Place the rum, Kahlúa, and Irish cream in a cocktail shaker, fill it two-thirds of the way with ice, and shake until chilled.

2. Strain over ice into a rocks glass, add the dash of crème de menthe, and garnish with the sprig of mint.

Slang Teacher

A trio of juices and coconut rum combine forces for a cocktail that's as fun as it is refreshing.

1. Add ice to a highball glass with ice and then add the coconut rum and juices.

2. Stir until chilled and garnish with the grapefruit twist.

1½ OZ. COCONUT RUM

1½ OZ. PINEAPPLE JUICE

¼ OZ. FRESH LEMON JUICE

3 OZ. GRAPEFRUIT JUICE

1 GRAPEFRUIT TWIST, FOR GARNISH

GLASSWARE:
HIGHBALL GLASS

½ OZ. FRESH LIME JUICE

2 OZ. COCONUT RUM

COLA, TO TOP

1 LIME WEDGE, FOR GARNISH

GLASSWARE:
MASON JAR

Privateer

You'll be surprised by the pleasant direction the substitution of coconut rum takes the Cuba Libre in.

1. Place the lime juice and rum in a mason jar filled with ice.

2. Fill the glass with cola, gently stir to combine, and garnish with the lime wedge.

When
I Come
Knocking

Rum forms the bridge between the whisky and brandy here, allowing the two bold flavors to accommodate one another.

1. Place the rum, whisky, brandy, and grenadine in a cocktail shaker, fill it two-thirds of the way with ice, and shake until chilled.

2. Strain over ice into a rocks glass and garnish with the maraschino cherry.

1 OZ. RUM

1 OZ. CROWN ROYAL WHISKY

1 OZ. BRANDY

SPLASH OF GRENADINE

1 MARASCHINO CHERRY, FOR GARNISH

GLASSWARE:
ROCKS GLASS

2 OZ. RUM

2 OZ. ORANGE JUICE

CLUB SODA, TO TOP

SPLASH OF GRENADINE

1 ORANGE SLICE, FOR GARNISH

GLASSWARE:
HIGHBALL GLASS

Red Rum

Far more pleasant than it looks in the mirror.

1. Add the rum and orange juice to a highball glass filled with ice and stir until chilled.

2. Top with the club soda and grenadine and garnish with the orange slice.

After Dark

A quality aged rum—such as Ron Zacapa—will work wonders here.

1. Add the rum and club soda to a highball glass filled with ice and gently stir until chilled.

2. Add the splash of grenadine and let it settle.

3. Top with the bitters and garnish with the lemon slice.

2 OZ. DARK RUM

4 OZ. CLUB SODA

½ OZ. GRENADINE

2 DROPS OF ANGOSTURA BITTERS

1 LEMON SLICE, FOR GARNISH

GLASSWARE:
HIGHBALL GLASS

2 OZ. DARK RUM

2 OZ. PINEAPPLE JUICE

2 OZ. ORANGE JUICE

2 DASHES OF ANGOSTURA BITTERS

1 PINEAPPLE SLICE, FOR GARNISH

GLASSWARE:
TUMBLER

Island Punch

Not the straight-ahead sipper the name would suggest, as the bitters add a lovely complexity.

1. Place the rum, juices, and bitters in a cocktail shaker, fill it two-thirds of the way with ice, and shake until chilled.

2. Strain over ice into a tumbler and garnish with the slice of pineapple.

Bow Tai

Cutting down the lengthy ingredient list of the Mai Tai to highlight the rum has myriad advantages.

1. Place the rums, Curaçao, and lime juice in a cocktail shaker, fill it two-thirds of the way with ice, and shake until chilled.

2. Strain over ice into a rocks glass and garnish with the lime wedge.

1½ OZ. WHITE RUM

¾ OZ. DARK RUM

¾ OZ. CURAÇAO

½ OZ. FRESH LIME JUICE

1 LIME WEDGE, FOR GARNISH

GLASSWARE:
ROCKS GLASS

1 OZ. COCONUT RUM

1 OZ. JÄGERMEISTER

4 OZ. APPLE JUICE OR APPLE CIDER

GROUND CINNAMON,
FOR GARNISH

GLASSWARE:
DOUBLE ROCKS GLASS

Ancora Tu

Jägermeister is thought of almost exclusively in terms of a shot, but its deep and varied flavor can come up big in cocktails.

1. Add the rum, Jägermeister, and juice or cider to a mixing glass, fill it two-thirds of the way with ice, and stir until chilled.

2. Strain over ice into a double rocks glass and garnish with a dusting of ground cinnamon.

Dark & Stormy

Fans are divided on whether the lime juice is sacrilege in this bold drink, so experiment with both preparations to see where you come down.

1. Place the rum, ginger beer, and lime juice in a rocks glass filled with ice and stir until chilled.

2. Garnish with the sprig of mint or lime wedge.

2 OZ. DARK RUM

4 OZ. GINGER BEER

½ OZ. FRESH LIME JUICE

1 SPRIG OF FRESH MINT OR LIME WEDGE, FOR GARNISH

GLASSWARE:
ROCKS GLASS

1 OZ. SPICED RUM

1 OZ. KAHLÚA

1 OZ. GRAND MARNIER

1 STRIP OF LEMON PEEL,
FOR GARNISH

GLASSWARE:
ROCKS GLASS

Dance This Mess Around

Like the B-52's classic, this one is a little bit all over the map, and nothing short of perfect.

1. Place the rum, Kahlúa, and Grand Marnier in a cocktail shaker, fill it two-thirds of the way with ice, and shake until chilled.

2. Strain over ice into a rocks glass and garnish with the strip of lemon peel.

Tom
& Jerry

If you're allergic to even the thought of eggnog, warm a bit of milk with the cinnamon stick and swap it in.

1. Place the syrup, rum, brandy, and warm eggnog in an Irish coffee glass and stir to combine.

2. Garnish with the cinnamon stick.

1 OZ. SIMPLE SYRUP (SEE PAGE 30)

1 OZ. DARK RUM

1 OZ. BRANDY

2 OZ. EGGNOG, WARMED

1 CINNAMON STICK, FOR GARNISH

GLASSWARE:
IRISH COFFEE GLASS

5 FRESH MINT LEAVES, TORN

¼ OZ. FRESH LIME JUICE

2 OZ. WHITE RUM

4 OZ. LEMONADE

1 LEMON WHEEL, FOR GARNISH

GLASSWARE:
ROCKS GLASS

Cool Summer

This one also works well as a batch cocktail. To make it for a group, simply quadruple the ingredients and place them in a pitcher.

1. Place the mint and lime juice in a rocks glass and muddle.

2. Add ice along with the rum and lemonade and stir until chilled.

3. Garnish with the lemon wheel.

Mary Pickford

The Luxardo is a late addition to this cocktail, which was conceived for the silent film star during the 1920s.

1. Chill a cocktail glass in the freezer.

2. Place the rum, juice, grenadine, and Luxardo in a cocktail shaker, fill it two-thirds of the way with ice, and shake until chilled.

3. Strain into the chilled glass and garnish with the cherries.

2 OZ. WHITE RUM

1½ OZ. PINEAPPLE JUICE

1 TEASPOON GRENADINE

6 DROPS OF LUXARDO
MARASCHINO LIQUEUR

2 MARASCHINO CHERRIES,
FOR GARNISH

GLASSWARE:
COCKTAIL GLASS

2 OZ. DARK RUM

1 OZ. PINEAPPLE JUICE

1 OZ. CREAM OF COCONUT

¾ OZ. SWEET VERMOUTH, TO FLOAT

1 SAGE LEAF, FOR GARNISH

GLASSWARE:
GOBLET OR WINE GLASS

The Penguin Cafe

You'll have to decide whether floating a bit of sweet vermouth atop a Painkiller is brilliant or madness.

1. Place the rum, pineapple juice, and cream of coconut in a cocktail shaker, fill it two-thirds of the way with ice, and shake until chilled.

2. Strain into a goblet or wine glass and float the vermouth on top by slowly pouring it into the drink.

3. Garnish with the sage leaf.

Caribbean Milk Punch

Consider Smith & Cross or Mt. Gay Black Barrel when selecting your rum for this one.

1. Place the rum, bourbon, syrup, and cream in a cocktail shaker, fill it two-thirds of the way with ice, and shake until chilled.

2. Strain into a coupe and garnish with a dusting of nutmeg.

1 OZ. AGED RUM

½ OZ. BOURBON

1 OZ. SIMPLE SYRUP (SEE PAGE 30)

1 OZ. HEAVY CREAM

FRESHLY GRATED NUTMEG, FOR GARNISH

GLASSWARE: COUPE

2 OZ. AGED RUM

½ OZ. AMARO NONINO
QUINTESSENTIA

½ OZ. APEROL

2 DASHES OF ANGOSTURA BITTERS

1 STRIP OF LEMON PEEL,
FOR GARNISH

GLASSWARE:
COCKTAIL GLASS

Indoor Pool

The delicate spice and citric sweetness of Amaro Nonino carry the day here.

1. Place the rum, amaro, Aperol, and bitters in a mixing glass, fill it two-thirds of the way with ice, and stir until chilled.

2. Strain into a cocktail glass and garnish with the strip of lemon peel.

Wines & Liqueurs

SUGAR, FOR THE RIM (OPTIONAL)

1½ OZ. COGNAC

¾ OZ. COINTREAU

¾ OZ. FRESH LEMON JUICE

1 LEMON TWIST, FOR GARNISH

GLASSWARE:
COUPE

Sidecar

Among Sidecar aficionados, much debate occurs over the Cointreau, with some reducing it to just enough to rinse the glass and others replacing it with Grand Marnier. If you want to get yours just so, focus your efforts there.

1. If desired, rim a coupe with sugar.

2. Place the Cognac, Cointreau, and lemon juice in a cocktail shaker, fill it two-thirds of the way with ice, and shake until chilled.

3. Strain into the coupe and garnish with the lemon twist.

Garibaldi

Bitter Campri entwines itself beautifully around an orange's sweetness.

1. Place 2 ice cubes in a goblet, add the Campari and a splash of orange juice, and stir to combine.

2. Add 1 more ice cube, fill the glass with more orange juice, and garnish with the orange twist.

1½ OZ. CAMPARI

FRESH ORANGE JUICE, TO TOP

1 ORANGE TWIST, FOR GARNISH

GLASSWARE: GOBLET

1 OZ. GREEN CRÈME DE MENTHE

1 OZ. WHITE CRÈME DE CACAO

1 OZ. HEAVY CREAM

GLASSWARE:
COCKTAIL GLASS

Grasshopper

Of all of the contributions New Orleans has made to the cocktail world, this may be the most impressive. Wherever one stands on that debate, they have to admit it's at least the most handsome.

1. Chill a cocktail glass in the freezer.

2. Place the ingredients in a cocktail shaker, fill it two-thirds of the way with ice, and shake until chilled.

3. Strain into the chilled glass.

Mimosa

3 OZ. ORANGE JUICE

A brunch classic. A 1-1 ratio of orange juice to Champagne is traditional, but can certainly be alerted in either direction to suit your taste.

3 OZ. CHAMPAGNE

1. Place the orange juice in a champagne flute and top with the Champagne.

GLASSWARE:
CHAMPAGNE FLUTE

2 OZ. PEACH NECTAR

¼ OZ. FRESH LEMON JUICE

CHAMPAGNE, TO TOP

**GLASSWARE:
CHAMPAGNE FLUTE**

Bellini

Peach nectar, which has a little bit of pulp, will make your Bellini a bit more luxurious than peach juice.

1. Place the peach nectar and lemon juice in a cocktail shaker, fill it two-thirds of the way with ice, and shake until chilled.

2. Strain into a champagne flute and top with Champagne.

Americano

When summer comes around, a dash of Suze will allow this drink's fans to remain by its side.

1. Add the Campari and vermouth to a highball glass with ice and stir to combine.

2. Top with club soda and garnish with the slice of orange.

1 OZ. CAMPARI

1 OZ. SWEET VERMOUTH

CLUB SODA, TO TOP

1 ORANGE SLICE, FOR GARNISH

GLASSWARE:
HIGHBALL GLASS

1½ OZ. ANGOSTURA BITTERS

½ OZ. RYE WHISKEY

¾ OZ. FRESH LEMON JUICE

1 OZ. ORGEAT

GLASSWARE:
COUPE

Trinidad Sour

Yes, that's a lot of bitters. But the excess opens the door to something unique, and transcendent.

1. Place all of the ingredients in a cocktail shaker, fill it two-thirds of the way with ice, and shake until chilled.

2. Strain into a coupe.

Son Shine

For this drink and the rest of your exotic liqueur needs, products from Giffard are always a good bet.

1. Chill a wine glass in the freezer.

2. Place the liqueur and wine in the chilled glass and stir to combine.

1 OZ. GIFFARD CRÈME DE PAMPLEMOUSSE ROSE

4 OZ. ROSÉ, CHILLED

GLASSWARE: WINE GLASS

1 TABLESPOON CASTER SUGAR

2 ORANGE SLICES

3½ OZ. AMONTILLADO OR OLOROSO
SHERRY

1 SPRIG OF FRESH MINT,
FOR GARNISH

GLASSWARE:
TIN CUP

Sherry Cobbler

If this isn't quite hitting the spot, try adding a dash of Luxardo maraschino liqueur to the mix.

1. Place the sugar and slices of orange in a cocktail shaker and muddle.

2. Add ice along with the sherry and shake until chilled.

3. Strain over crushed ice into a tin cup and garnish with the sprig of mint.

Sakura Martini

If you can't track down an in-season cherry blossom, an olive will do for the garnish.

1. Place the sake, gin, and Luxardo in a mixing glass, fill it two-thirds of the way with ice, and stir until chilled.

2. Strain into a cocktail glass and garnish with the cherry blossom.

2½ OZ. DRY SAKE

1 OZ. GIN

¼ TEASPOON LUXARDO
MARASCHINO LIQUEUR

1 CHERRY BLOSSOM, FOR GARNISH

GLASSWARE:
COCKTAIL GLASS

2 OZ. FINO SHERRY

· ·

¾ OZ. GRAND MARNIER

· ·

When the Snow Falls

A surprisingly festive cocktail made for staring out a window as the snow falls against the light of a streetlamp.

1. Place the sherry and Grand Marnier in a mixing glass, fill it two-thirds of the way with ice, and gently stir until chilled.

2. Strain into a coupe.

GLASSWARE:
COUPE

Lipstick & Rouge

The unlikely pairing of Aperol and amaretto is certain to provide a pleasant surprise to all who come in contact with this effervescent cocktail.

1. Place the Aperol, amaretto, and lemon juice in a cocktail shaker, fill it two-thirds of the way with ice, and shake until chilled.

2. Strain into a champagne flute, top with the Prosecco, and garnish with the lemon twist.

¾ OZ. APEROL

¾ OZ. AMARETTO

¾ OZ. FRESH LEMON JUICE

3 OZ. PROSECCO

1 LEMON TWIST, FOR GARNISH

GLASSWARE:
CHAMPAGNE FLUTE

1 OZ. BLUE CURAÇAO

1 OZ. IRISH CREAM

1 OZ. GIFFARD BANANE DU BRÉSIL

GLASSWARE:
COUPE

Blue Monday

Any curaçao will work here, but blue lends the drink a positively wild color.

1. Place the ingredients in a cocktail shaker, fill it two-thirds of the way with ice, and shake until chilled.

2. Strain into a coupe.

Emerald Isle

Three of Ireland's finest exports get combined in this luscious crowd-pleaser.

1. Fill a pint glass three-quarters of the way with the Guinness.

2. Fill a shot glass with the whiskey and the Irish cream.

3. Drop the shot glass into the pint glass, and, since the Irish cream will curdle, drink as fast as you can.

12 OZ. GUINNESS STOUT

¾ OZ. IRISH WHISKEY

¾ OZ. IRISH CREAM

GLASSWARE:
PINT GLASS

1 OZ. PEPPERMINT SCHNAPPS

1 OZ. KAHLÚA

1 OZ. IRISH CREAM

GLASSWARE:
ROCKS GLASS

After Five

Not particularly fancy, but delicious, and plenty of fun.

1. Add the ingredients to a rocks glass containing ice in the order they are listed and stir until chilled.

Headlights Look Like Diamonds

A charming riff on the classic Kir Cocktail.

1. Pour the liqueurs into a champagne flute, top with Champagne, and garnish with a grapefruit twist.

½ OZ. ST-GERMAIN

1 OZ. GIFFARD CRÈME DE PAMPLEMOUSSE ROSE

CHAMPAGNE, TO TOP

1 GRAPEFRUIT TWIST, FOR GARNISH

GLASSWARE: CHAMPAGNE FLUTE

3 OZ. PERNOD

....

1 OZ. FRESH LEMON JUICE

....

TONIC WATER, TO TOP

....

Sweet Pea

Lower in licorice flavor than other members of the pastis family, the lemon juice lifts Pernod's lovely and numerous herbal notes to the fore.

1. Add the Pernod and lemon juice to a cocktail shaker, fill it two-thirds of the way with ice, and shake until chilled.

2. Strain into a coupe and top with tonic water.

GLASSWARE:
COUPE

The Last Word

Make one and put on Bill Evans's "Peace Piece" for company.

1. Chill a coupe in the freezer.

2. Place the Chartreuse, Luxardo, gin, and lime juice in a cocktail shaker, fill it two-thirds of the way with ice, and shake until chilled.

3. Strain into the chilled coupe and garnish with the lime twist.

½ OZ. CHARTREUSE

½ OZ. LUXARDO MARASCHINO LIQUEUR

½ OZ. GIN

½ OZ. FRESH LIME JUICE

1 MARASCHINO CHERRY, FOR GARNISH

GLASSWARE:
COUPE

1½ OZ. CYNAR

½ OZ. CHARTREUSE

¾ OZ. FRESH LIME JUICE

½ OZ. DEMERARA SYRUP
(SEE PAGE 30)

14 DROPS OF ANGOSTURA BITTERS,
FOR GARNISH

GLASSWARE:
COCKTAIL GLASS

Drink of Laughter and Forgetting

A drink as bittersweet and profound as its title suggests.

1. Place the Cynar, Chartreuse, lime juice, and syrup in a cocktail shaker, fill it two-thirds of the way with ice, and shake until chilled.

2. Strain into a cocktail glass and garnish with the bitters.

Old Hickory

An all-out assault on vermouth's tendency to be overlooked by modern drinkers.

1. Add the vermouths and bitters to a rocks glass filled halfway with ice, stir until chilled, and garnish with the lemon twist.

1½ OZ. DRY VERMOUTH

1½ OZ. SWEET VERMOUTH

2 DASHES OF PEYCHAUD'S BITTERS

DASH OF ORANGE BITTERS

1 LEMON TWIST, FOR GARNISH

GLASSWARE:
ROCKS GLASS

1½ OZ. AQUAVIT

½ OZ. FRESH LIME JUICE

½ OZ. ORGEAT

1 EGG WHITE

1 SORREL LEAF, FOR GARNISH

GLASSWARE:
COUPE

Early Start

Aquavit is gaining momentum with the world's top bartenders, thanks to its ability to work well with bold flavors.

1. Place the aquavit, lime juice, orgeat, and egg white in a cocktail shaker containing no ice and dry shake for 15 seconds.

2. Add ice to the shaker and shake until chilled.

3. Double-strain into a coupe and garnish with the sorrel leaf.

SAN FRANCISCO WORLD SPIRITS COMPETITION 2012 DOUBLE GOLD
FESTLIG
AQUAVIT
KROGSTAD
DISTILLED FROM GRAIN

Green Goddess Punch

"The green fairy" has lost some of her sinister reputation, opening the door to delicious drinks such as this.

1. Add the absinthe, lime juice, and syrup to a tumbler filled with ice and stir to combine.

2. Top with the Topo Chico and garnish with the lemon twist.

1 OZ. ABSINTHE

1 OZ. FRESH LIME JUICE

1 OZ. SIMPLE SYRUP (SEE PAGE 30)

4 OZ. TOPO CHICO

1 LEMON TWIST, FOR GARNISH

GLASSWARE:
TUMBLER

3 OZ. PINEAPPLE JUICE

1 OZ. CREAM OF COCONUT

1 OZ. HEAVY CREAM

2 OZ. CAMPARI

1 ORANGE SLICE, FOR GARNISH

GLASSWARE:
HURRICANE GLASS

Campari Colada

Think about it: Would this beverage have made it all the way to you if it weren't uniquely delicious?

1. Place the pineapple juice, cream of coconut, cream, and Campari in a blender, add ½ cup ice, and puree until combined.

2. Pour into a Hurricane glass and garnish with the orange slice.

Apple Blossom

Like The White Stripes' album this song appears on, *De Stijl*, this cocktail has a small, but rabid following.

1. Add the applejack, St-Germain, and lime juice to a double rocks glass filled with ice, stir until chilled, and top with seltzer water.

1½ OZ. APPLEJACK

½ OZ. ST-GERMAIN

½ OZ. FRESH LIME JUICE

SELTZER WATER, TO TOP

GLASSWARE:
DOUBLE ROCKS GLASS

Metric Conversions

US Measurement	Approximate Metric Liquid Measurement	Approximate Metric Dry Measurement
1 teaspoon	5 ml	5 g
1 tablespoon or ½ ounce	15 ml	14 g
1 ounce or ⅛ cup	30 ml	29 g
¼ cup or 2 ounces	60 ml	57 g
⅓ cup	80 ml	76 g
½ cup or 4 ounces	120 ml	113 g
⅔ cup	160 ml	151 g
¾ cup or 6 ounces	180 ml	170 g
1 cup or 8 ounces or ½ pint	240 ml	227 g
1½ cups or 12 ounces	350 ml	340 g
2 cups or 1 pint or 16 ounces	475 ml	454 g
3 cups or 1½ pints	700 ml	680 g
4 cups or 2 pints or 1 quart	950 ml	908 g

Index

About Cider Mill Press Book Publishers

Good ideas ripen with time. From seed to harvest, Cider Mill Press brings fine reading, information, and entertainment together between the covers of its creatively crafted books. Our Cider Mill bears fruit twice a year, publishing a new crop of titles each spring and fall.

"Where Good Books Are Ready for Press"

Visit us online at
cidermillpress.com

or write to us at

PO Box 454
12 Spring St.
Kennebunkport, Maine 04046